Image is important,

Bill

Conversations with Entrepreneurs

With contributing authors

Garrett Gunderson

Joel Comm

Bill Hoffer

Chuck Kammer

Grace Stephens

Jeff Roldan

Marvin Montillano

Stacy Kirch

Stephanie Landers

Sara McKay

Jason Cotter

Woody Woodward

D.U. Publishing
39252 Winchester Road #107-430
Murrieta, CA 92563

www.dupublishing.com

Warning – Disclaimer

The purpose of this book is to educate and inspire. This book is not intended to give advice or make promises or guarantees that anyone following the ideas, tips, suggestions, techniques or strategies will have the same results as the people listed throughout the stories contained herein. The author, publisher and distributor(s) shall have neither liability nor responsibility to anyone with respect to any loss or damage caused, or alleged to be caused, directly or indirectly by the information contained in this book.

ISBN 0-9785802-7-3

Table of Contents

Introduction

Have you ever wanted to be a sitting in the room while someone you admired was being interviewed? Have you ever wanted to be the "fly on the wall" just to hear what they are really saying about success, happiness and life? I too have always wanted that and this is why I developed Conversations with Entrepreneurs. There are so many books out there that are too polished and do not get down to the nitty gritty on how to succeed. With this book series I structured the book so it would feel as if you were right there in the conversation. It is not overly polished or perfected but it is real and true. Join with me as I interview some of the top entrepreneurs of our time. Some are New York Times best selling authors and some are just like you and me.

I hope you enjoy these conversations and I invite you to fill out the questionnaire at the back of the book. It is set up in an interview format. Maybe next time I will interview you. Till then...

Sincerely,
David E. Chambers

Chapter 1

Garrett Gunderson

Financial Visionary – New York Times Bestseller

David E. Chambers (Chambers)
Garrett, what inspired you to get into your type of work?

Garrett Gunderson (Gunderson):
When I was 15 years old, I had a car detailing business. There was nothing original as far as the name goes – just Garrett Gunderson's Car Care! I only had a net income of $600 with the first few months of being in business, but I presented it at a Business Competition and won $500. The next year, I did the same thing; only, I took first for the State of Utah, and won $5,000. It's interesting – here I was, a sixteen

year old who had won $5,000, but immediately I wanted to invest it…
that was my inclination. I thought, "Okay! I'm going to invest." First
of all, I'm from a small town-place in Utah. So, I thought I was rich
when I won $5,000! But, as I went out looking and talking and ask-
ing people about where I should invest it, I got all sorts of different
opinions; when it was time to seriously invest, no one wanted to help
because I had to have a custodian to help me. My parents would have
to sign off saying that it was okay. For most of these brokers and in-
vestment advisors, $5,000 wasn't of enough interest to them.

When I was eighteen, I finally had a firm which said, "Yes, we'll
help you out. Just put in $70 a month into this little product. It's going
to earn 18% a year, and you're going to be a multi-millionaire 40 years
from now." That wasn't true – even though I did it. Three months later,
when I was enquiring and asking and figuring about if this was the
best thing, I was offered an internship with the financial firm. So, I
went to college, worked in Finances, and as I went through trying to
help people out financially, what I recognized was that just getting
them the right products or helping them be more efficient didn't al-
ways make a difference to their happiness because it was about their
mindset.

So, what inspired me to do what I do now was really a mixture of
helping people with self-development – because I personally paid
a tremendous amount of money on coaching, mentoring and self-
development over my life – but I made sure that they had a path that
could be implemented in their life, which was about financial trans-
actions and bringing a marriage between the two. It was awesome
to watch people get that – have them invest, to be a good expression
of who they are, manage their risks because of a concept I call 'Soul
Purpose', and really start to have a measurable difference in their

life and happiness.

So, my inspiration came through personal experience and constant enquiry, and then really getting clear about the fact that that was a gift that I had in my life… and that really brought about the passion.

Chambers:

That is really a very unique story! Why, at sixteen, did you not just go out and buy a car, just like any other sixteen year-old, or go out on a trip and have a good time? What was the driving force that made you say, "I need to take this money and invest it"?

Gunderson:

At the time, there was both good and bad to it. Internally, I looked at it and said, "Okay! What can I do to better my situation? What can I do to have this help me move forward and be more successful?"

On the external side, I thought, "Man! If I'm a millionaire, do you know how cool that would be and what people would think about me? Wouldn't that mean that I really made it?" So, I was really motivated by improving my situation.

One way was a very powerful way of improving it; the other way, as I found out, was a very limited way and it really impacted the first few years of my life, when I was right out of college and in my career. But once again, it brought about new experiences and new inspiration to make a big difference in the world.

Chambers:

What was the defining event that happened, when you realized that you were being external with the money and internal with your passion?

Gunderson:

I can remember two specific things that brought about the clarity. When I first graduated college and I was making six figures in my first year out of college, I remember thinking, "Okay! I want to be a millionaire, because once I'm a millionaire, I'm going to be so happy!" It was more like an 'if and then' scenario which was deferring my life.

So, I was living in an apartment and yet, I owned fourteen other apartments which I rented to other people. So, I didn't own my own place, but I owned places for other people. My wife had just graduated college – at that time, she was my soon-to-be wife – and I didn't want her to buy any new clothes, because that was going to hurt our net worth. So, here she was, soon going to be a teacher – a third grade school teacher and then, a first grade school teacher the next year – and I didn't want her to buy new clothes. Now the clothes we wear in college aren't necessarily professional suits which are good when you're teaching kids.

So, what I recognized through a conversation with my father was that that was a really limited mindset. I was in the car with my dad and I remember telling my dad, "Dad, I've got a motto in life and I think it's brilliant. I'm going to work like no one else will work today, and then in the future, I'm going to live like no one else can live." I though that that was perfect! My dad looked over at me and said, "Son, are you ever going to be able to recover or recapture the memories you lose along the way?" And that just hit me. I thought, "Wow!" and for a while, I just sat with it.

I hadn't fully grasped what my dad was saying yet, but shortly after that, I was at an event in Las Vegas – it was for the Top Investment and Insurance professionals in the world. Here I was at a young age, going to this event in Las Vegas, and I remember going out into the hallway and running into a woman who I had a lot of respect for in the industry... she was well-known, she was in the top 1% of the company she worked for in earnings. I engaged in a conversation with her and she told me about a program that she went through on self-development that I'd gone through too. I said, "I thought it was okay!" to which she said, "Only okay, huh?" And then she said, "That's probably more about you, than it is about the program."

I was a little taken aback... I said, "What do you mean?" She said, "Well, look at your life – what do you accept as 'this is the way life is', without creating it that way? What do you accept as is?" At that moment, I chose to just be honest. That's a tough thing to do for a lot of people – to just be honest about that situation, because we're enamored with looking good and here was someone I respected. I told her that we lived in an apartment even though we could afford a house, even though my wife wanted to live in a house; I told her that we're just going to sacrifice this way for a few years... and I just kept talking for about 15 minutes with her listening to me.

And she got it – she saw what I couldn't see. She said, "What are you fighting? What if you just put yourself in your wife's shoes? What is it like being married to you in regards to freedom?" And it hit me like a ton of bricks! I said, "I'm totally controlling! I'm letting some abstract thought limit our enjoyment today" You have to understand that when we did go on vacation, I would spend less money on food than when we were at home because that might hurt our net worth! I assessed every dollar I spent. I obsessed about money all too often and it was clouding me. What's interesting is that in that moment, I called my wife immediately. I was in Las Vegas with thousands of people at the workshop and all of a sudden, I was in the hallway admitting my limitation and breaking down and crying... even though there were all these people walking around me, I didn't even care because I was apologizing and I was creating a new opportunity of a more loving marriage and a co-creative marriage where we live the life we want now, and we turn that someday into 'that' day. No more living into the future of 'One day we will be happy' and 'One day this will all work out'! We said, "What can we do today?"

And within three months, we were in our dream home, and in twelve months, I was making three times more money–remember, I was already making six figures – just letting go of a limited belief and this controlling philosophy of trying to be a millionaire which was so out there… it was so outside of me. It was all about money and accounts; not about out happiness. It wasn't about value creation. And what I ended up finding is that even though I was doing the same work, I enjoyed it a hundred times more because I wasn't so focused on myself. I could actually look at the client and their situation from a new set of eyes.

Chambers:

It sounds like you took action at a pivotal time in your life where things were against you and things were difficult. You made a conscious decision to change. Why do you think other people don't take action?

Gunderson:

There are a few reasons why many people don't take action. The first reason is because people get into a situation where they don't know exactly what to do, and they let FEAR – as in False Evidence Appearing Real – make decisions for them through inaction. They pause; they stop. I think the reason why that fear comes about is that they wonder how they're going to look if they admit how they really feel and the uncertainty that they truly have out in the world... if they tell someone else, "I don't have the answer" or "I don't know" or say, "Can you help me?" People who feel like they've been successful or they should be successful, or define success by what others think, get stuck in inaction because they're so addicted to how they appear to that person that they won't admit what really is. We can never progress until we're willing to be honest and we're willing to say, "This is what is actually going on right now."

So for me, I call my mentors... I call the people that I want to look best to, and I say, "You know what? I don't know why I'm in this situation; I thought I learnt the first time! I can't see past the problem because I'm in the problem." As Einstein said, "We're never going to get out of our problems with the same thinking that got us there in the first place." I engage in conversations where someone is willing to ask me the powerful question.

Chambers:

I know that you've used mentors throughout your entire career. What does it take to find a good mentor?

Gunderson:

I'm a huge advocate of mentors because first of all, I spend more money on mentoring and coaching now than I did when I began my career. I have more responsibilities and at times there is more complexity... there's more I don't know than what I realized before. So, I'm looking for people who are experts. What I've looked for in a mentor is someone who's actually practicing what they preach. I'm not looking for an advisor who tells me what to do. I'm pretty intelligent – I can figure out what to do when given the right question or the right framing or context. Now, I can make powerful choices because they bring an awareness to me by asking proper questions.

> *Number One: Mentor's have to be confident enough to ask the question*

> *Number Two: They live what they're talking about – they live what they teach. That's what makes them a mentor.*

Also, when I look at the different mentors that I have, they aren't just teaching in the industry that they're talking about; they've been extraordinarily successful in their own right. So, I can see their ventures and the companies these people work for. They have an expertise there, because they were profitable. This is something that they do.

I don't look for reactive mentors, meaning those who are just talking about what is happening at the moment. I look for the creators – the pioneers – who are the ones moving forward. They're the ones who are forging and building this path, and they have no fear of me and my power. Some people aren't willing to call me on my own crap because they don't want to hurt my feelings; but I love the person who says, "Garrett, what's really going on? What's the real story? Let's get to the core here so that we can see how to improve the situation.

Chambers:

What does it take to be a good mentor? A lot of times, we have an opportunity to mentor somebody and we've never been taught how to mentor.

Gunderson:

> *Number One: You have to be willing to listen.*

Number Two: *You have to ask the question behind the question.*

So, as a mentor, let's say if someone teaches you that 'this' is a powerful question, asking that one powerful question may well be the first layer that's peeled back to get more to the core. You have to be able to be in that moment and by listening and hearing the response, be asking the question that delves even deeper. From there, I'm going to give four specific keys that I see in mentoring.

Number One: *You have to be committed to your own lifelong education and be able to teach as well.*

Mentors don't stop learning – they continue to have mentors themselves. Some of the mentors may not have their personal mentors, and I'm scared of that type of mentor. It may not be the same type of relationship – Woody, I consider you a mentor, and I know that you have consideration areas when I'm a mentor.

Number Two: *You have to have systems and tools to reinforce that education*

Number Three: *Accountability – you have to have systems of accountability and be able to hold someone accountable.*

Number Four: *You have to be willing to ask questions. You have to be willing to be a mentor instead of an advisor.*

Chambers:

When you get discouraged and feel low, what do you do to pull yourself out of it?

Gunderson:

There are a few simple things that I do.

Number One: *It's absolutely essential that I work out. I have to workout. If I get discouraged and get down, I work out.*

Number Two: *I admit to someone who's important, especially a mentor, that I am discouraged, and that I am frustrated.*

Number Three: I like to write and create a new plan, or create a big commitment which is bigger than my discouragement. So, if I'm discouraged because something didn't work out, I use that and say, "What can I learn from that situation?" Rather than be distracted or derailed or limited to that situation, I ask myself, "What vision is so big that that distraction, or that disappointment, seems small?" And then, it's time for me to create anew.

Chambers:

How do you stay focused on your business when there are so many things pulling at you? You're a New York Times Bestseller, you've got your beautiful family and wonderful children, you're traveling and coaching, and there are all these things you do for society and your charitable work... how do you stay focused on the task at hand?

Gunderson:

I have to admit that it's not always easy to be able to commit the time I want for my family, to become a New York Times bestseller... there were times when I found myself out of balance, but this was the key.

I had an awareness that I was out of balance, and I asked myself, "Is this what I want? What can I do about it?"

The power of being out of balance is that I started to ask how I could be more effective, how I could be more efficient and resourceful. Who was the team that I could rely on? How could I use more technology? How could I use the media and filming to replicate myself, better than just meeting one-on-one? That is what I do when I find myself trying to refocus on my businesses. I ask, "How can I make the same impact with less effort? How can I utilize the gifts I personally have and the gifts that the people on my team have, and start to delegate the situation?"

I always go back to the five things that I love to do the most in business. If I'm not doing those five things for the majority of my time, once again I have a retreat for a day or two. I bring my team and find out how I can refocus and how I can delegate, so that I can go back into what's most important, rather than what's most pressing at the moment.

Chambers:

You're very good at analyzing your own life, correcting yourself when you're off-course. Is there a routine that you have, or something you do in the mornings, afternoons and evenings, that keeps you in line with what you do?

Gunderson:

I call it a Producer Power Hour. I like to spend a minimum of one hour, the first thing in the morning. When you go to sleep, you've been in darkness, haven't eaten and your body's still in more of a coma state. For me, it's not the exact energy that I have later on in the day.

So, I begin by doing some exercise. After exercise, I like to listen to something on my iPod that mentally intrigues me. That might programs by my spiritual mentors and teachers, or it might just be that I'm listening to a book on tape, or I'm listening to someone who's an expert in marketing because that is what I'm focusing on, in my business.

After I finish listening to my iPod which I usually listen to, on the way to the gym and on the way home from the gym; if I'm working out on my own, I might even listen to it while I'm at the gym – I go to my meditation room and focus on being calm and being grounded in my spirituality. I like to meditate, I like to pray a little bit, and then say a statement or a declaration of what I'm committed to accomplishing that day which is in alignment with who I am and my principles.

After I finish those three focuses, I'm ready to go out for the day. I'm ready to go because I've created a good space for abundance, and I've created favorable conditions for me to create the best expression of who I am – that is what I call Soul Purpose.

Chambers:

Tell us a little more about Soul Purpose?

Gunderson:

Soul Purpose is something that every single person uniquely has in the world, without exception and without fail. Whether people recognize it and live it and express it, is another thing. Soul Purpose is a combination of your multiple talents and abilities and gifts, and that combination is now combined with the things that ignite the most passion as you do them.

So, you have a Soul Purpose that can be expressed in business, your Soul Purpose can be expressed with your family – it's really who you are. Any time that you are not being who you are – which a lot of people do on a regular basis, because they can't really answer who they are in the first place – you're not living your Soul Purpose.

So, at the core, it's who we truly are, and it's our god-given talents and abilities. As we recognize it, we find power in life and we find a real expression of joy.

Chambers:

How does someone identify with their Soul Purpose?

Gunderson:

There are a few ways to do that. The first would be to just do the Producer Power Hour I talked about, each and every morning, because it creates some space for you. The second thing is to simply take time, and look deeper internally. Think about who you are, and what you're capable of. I think meditation is a good source for that.

There are also a few other things that you can do like finding out what your natural inclination is with personality tests. But, don't take it as your Soul Purpose – use it as a guide and start to synthesize it, until you get a completely clear and concise statement about what that Soul Purpose is and who you are.

My Soul Purpose is to help other people uncover and discover their Soul Purpose. That's the best way of expressing my Soul Purpose – whether that's me being a parent, or me being a business partner, or whether that's me working with a client. That is a good expression of my Soul Purpose.

I've created exercises for people so that they can say, ' I find myself happiest when…', 'I find myself most creative when…', 'I find that I get the most compliments when I'm doing this' and then brainstorming those. Your Soul Purpose is not any one of those activities, but the combination of those activities shows a good way for you to express that. You can even go to people who know you pretty well–what do they see as your abilities? What do they see as your Soul Purpose?

What you'll find is that most people discount their sole purpose and their abilities because it came very naturally to them. They think, "Everyone's good at that!" But that isn't true. You're great at that; stop looking at what other people are so great at and having any envy. Instead look at what you can contribute and what's unique to you. As you do that, align that with the things that bring forth the most passion. So, build the right vision for your life; build the biggest context which is a cause worthy for your life. That's the most I can give in this short period of time.

We actually have events called 'Soul Purpose Intensives', where we do things to help people find their Soul Purpose as a part of our coaching program.

Chambers:

If people wanted to learn more about their Soul Purpose, how could they contact you for that information?

Gunderson:

The best way to contact me personally would be going to www.garrettbgunderson.com. There are many ways to get involved with us. You can email us to figure out what's going on now. That would be my recommendation right now.

Chambers:

What was it like to turn your passion and dream into a New York Times *bestseller?*

Gunderson:

It was not the easiest journey. At the time, I had a business partner named Les McGuire. We sat down one day and said, "Let's get a book out there. There's a book in you somewhere, and I have a way of pulling information out of you and organize it and contribute to it. So, we're going to do this book together." We had scheduled some time for late June '06 at a hotel so that we could go and spend time there. He had scheduled some time before that just to get his ideas down and think through it himself.

In early June, he died in a plane crash. Now, we had made a declaration to our firm that we were going to produce this book, and after the plane crash, I almost forgot about the book for some time. I started to get caught up in keeping things alive, and in survival, and just trying to handle things for two different partners who had died at the same firm. I found myself going away from the things that I loved to do and actually found myself getting out of balance in life.

I got to the point where I wasn't the one who could get up, go to the front of the room and speak, and tell them, "Hey! These are the things you should do in life. These are the principles you should follow." because I felt that I was personally violating them.

In November '06, I brought the firm together and said, "I can no longer operate the way we are operating. I don't feel we're creating the right value, I don't think this is the direction we want to go in. I'm going back to the business that I've created in Salt Lake City – this other firm that I was trying to take over for was in Provo–and I'm going to take 30 days to get clear about what my purpose is."

In those 30 days, we wrote more of the book than I had written in the previous two years. I had got about 72 pages done before that. We scrapped most of those, got a lot of the book done in those 30 days, and then it only took three months past that to really get it refined and complete the first round of edits. We were going to self-publish and put the book out there. I was at an event, and I had invited everyone to this event, and I got up and said, "I commit to being a New York Times best seller within the next 12 months!" One of my business partners was in the room and he was really inspired by that. He said, "That's great! Are you really serious about that?" I said, "I'm very serious about it." So, he said, "I'm going to call one of my clients who is a brilliant marketer and I'm going to ask him what it takes."

His friend said, "I don't really know how to do that in the book industry, but I can locate whoever's the best at it." When he did, I got on the phone with that person, and I said, "Alright! This is what I've committed to." He said, "Great! My fee is $95,000 to be your book promoter, your literary agent and to help you actually better your book."

I said, "What do you mean? I've already got a great book." He then asked me about 10 questions which made me realize that although my book was good, it didn't appeal to all the different types of personas, or the different types of readers. I didn't have a real marketing plan; I just had $5,000. He said, "Let's get you published." Within a week, we got published and I thought, "We've got most of the hard work done!"

Interestingly enough, the journey really began there because at this point, it took more work in editing and redoing the book than composing the first version from scratch. He was dedicating a lot of time and just two weeks after hiring him, I had two real estate partners tell me that they were incurring bankruptcy. I inherited a portfolio of real estate that was not preferable. I had to go through the whole working-with-the-attorneys to get this restructured and taken over, because I didn't want them to have to go through the whole bankruptcy process. It started to distract me – there was just one distraction after the other, but I had made this commitment.

So, even as I had some ill-equity based upon my real estate, at the same time, I had committed to hire a PR rep from New York for $91,000 with one of the largest book promoting firms. I had committed to having a full page ad promoting my book out in the New York Times, and the cover of Publishers' Weekly. I had committed to hiring a consulting firm to revamp how our businesses would operate to fulfill and facilitate. We could just go on and on and on... but the thing is that I had made a public declaration and I was committed to my word. I was also committed to being greater than my circumstance.

So, at that time, it was seemingly impossible to bring about a New York Times bestseller, because I had to travel to LA and New York and Chicago to do the different events in the midst of all these different interruptions in my business. I was trying to maintain a balance with my life at the same time – there were even days within the last year when I had $0 in my bank account, and yet I had to make a flight and have a hotel booked. People stepped up to my life because I was honest, and because I was committed to my word. I was committed to that 'greater than the circumstances I was facing' approach... and it happened! It came about!

So, if you're passionate enough, and are clear and 100% committed to that vision, you can bring forth something as great as having a New York Times bestseller. During the time when we launched our book, business books were struggling with sales. We did great with sales – we hit Number One with USA Today for the Money Section; we hit the New York Times for not only the 'How-To', but also for Business. So, we hit two different lists with New York Times; we hit the Wall Street Journal List; we hit Number Two all over with Amazon.com, just behind the little vampire book by Stephanie Myers. We hit Number One for Business and Economics and all these different things; but it was a level of commitment, even in the face of dire circumstances that pulled us through.

Chambers:

What advice would you give to a young entrepreneur who wants to go out and make it in the world?

Gunderson:

I was an entrepreneur by the age of 15 with an official business, with official business licenses; but it wasn't necessarily sexy or savvy! It was a start and it got me going. It got me to think creatively about how I could do business better and how I could do it differently. Eventually, the question which came up was, "How can I create something that didn't exist before?" which was an even more powerful question.

Anyone can be an entrepreneur. Not everyone chooses to be an entrepreneur, but we all are entrepreneurs because all of us have our Soul Purpose. It's our responsibility to be productive with that. My recommendation is – don't let anyone say that you can't do business unless you golf; I don't golf. Don't let anyone tell you that you can't do business unless you dress a certain way; you should have seen how I dressed early on in business and even how my hair looked! Don't let people tell you that you're too old, or you're too young, or that you don't have a degree and a designation.

You don't have to have a degree or a designation – what you have to have is the vision and a commitment to that vision. You've just take action and recognize – there will be things that happen along the way that you wouldn't have planned for, that you wouldn't have said, "I want this to happen". They're going to happen anyway. But when you're committed to that vision, you're going to say, "I'm going to learn a lesson from that. I'm going to use that as a part of my story. I'm going to use that as an ingredient to move forward. Some of the best businesses ever created were because one of those things came along. They figured out a way to resolve that and then they taught other people to go ahead and go for it – to just do it.

It's not just about textbooks, although you must commit yourself to education; it's about your personal beliefs and your belief that you can make a difference. Find out what it is that inspires you to go that and go for it! Do it! It's available to you! That's where the real wealth is – people who get to live, and do what they want to do in business. That's better than any stock.

The person who created the business is the person who profits the most. Whether it's issuing stock or a piece of real estate, the person who runs the business around that is the one really profiting from real estate, or whatever that business is. Make sure it's something that you are really inspired by, and that it's a good contribution with who you are.

Chambers:

What legacy do you want to leave?

Gunderson:

The legacy that I want to leave is that by the end of my lifetime, the financial institutions do business completely differently – they look at individuals and they have to understand something about who they are, and not who they are in relation to risk tolerance or any of the things that you hear today. But they understand what contribution they want to make and what difference they want to make. It's not just about the rate of return; it's about designing products that help people express who they are.

And so, I want to revolutionize the financial industry so that people aren't so focused on money; they're focused on real wealth which is finance, Soul Purpose, mentality, physical wellbeing and social impact. That's the wealth I want people to recognize and live beyond just having money be their primary reason or excuse for life.

For more information, visit:

www.garrettbgunderson.com

Chapter 2

Joel Comm

Internet and marketing Genius – New York Times Bestseller

David E. Chambers (Chambers)
Joel, how did you get started in your line of work?

Joel Comm (Comm):

I've always been into computers – I was sixteen years old when I bought a TRS 80 Model 1 from Radio Shack. I just had an interest in computers – not because I wanted to be a programmer, but because I thought that there was power, and that this was the future.

In 1995, I built my first website called www.worldvillage.com. It was a software review site that would review computer games and educational software from a parent's perspective. It wasn't just about how fun the game was, but also how appropriate it would be for children. In 1996, I partnered with a programmer in California named Guinness Masters at the University of California, San Diego. He had developed the foundation for multi-player game rooms where people could play hearts, spades, chess, checkers, bridge, backgammon and those types of table and card games against other people on the internet in real time. He only had a few people playing then. So, I said, "Why don't we partner up, re-brand it and see what we can build here?" We did and we called it www.classicgames.com and today, the site is known as Yahoo Games. Yahoo acquired it from us in 1997 and re-branded it. That was my first really big joint venture online.

Then, I rode the internet wave up to the top – from that time forward to the year 2000. The bubble just got bigger and bigger, and the money was just crazy online. And then, I rode back down when the bubble burst in late 2000. I hung with it – I laid off just about everybody except myself, but I hung with it because I felt it was going to come back again.

And in 2004, it did… and it came back thanks to the likes of Google who launched a program called Google AdSense which allowed any website owner to place Google Ads on their website and get a share of the revenue from Google. So, in a few months, I went from making just $20 or $30 a day, to $500 to $1,000 a day in passive income with Google AdSense. I told some of my friends and associates about how I was doing it and they suggested that I write a book on the topic. So, I created an e-book which we released at the beginning of the year 2005 – 'What Google Never Told You about Making Money with AdSense'. It was an instant hit. We made $10,000 in the first week selling a $77 e-book. Word began to spread and sales just picked up, and before you know it, I was known as the AdSense Guru online – the guy who knew how to make money with content-based websites.

That turned into a physical book called 'The AdSense Code', which was released in spring of 2006. That went on to become a New York Times bestseller, and since that time, we've done a lot of different projects. Last year, I produced the world's first competitive internet reality show, which is called 'The Next Internet Millionaire'. I also recently came out with a book called 'Click Here to Order – Stories of the World's Most Successful Internet Marketing Entrepreneurs', which hit Amazon's, and Barnes and Nobles' bestseller list.

Now, we're diversifying into other areas of technology such as developing applications for the iPhone, and we're getting ready to launch a mobile marketing service that people will be able to use to market to people on their cell phones. My wife says that I'm a little ADD, and I get distracted by the bright shiny objects... but we're building a business here that does a lot of different things using technology, and teaching people how they can leverage their technology to build a business that can replace their JOB.

Chambers:

That is an amazing story! What was it like selling to Yahoo? The first couple of times when you sit down with them, the numbers are big and in your mind, you go, "This can be huge!" What was that like?

Comm:

It was really interesting actually. We had contacted a lot of Search Engines, contacted Exide, Lycos, and Infoseek – of course, these are names from the Dinosaur Age of the Internet – even AOL and some online game services... none of them were really interested, especially the search engines. The search engines were really focused on search. Then one day, I got an email from Yahoo without any solicitation saying that they were interested in investigating partnerships with us. My partner was already in San Diego, California and I was in Oklahoma at the time – or actually Texas – and we went out to Yahoo in San Jose. There, I spotted David Filo walking around the office barefoot, and met some of their management team. We sat down with them and they wanted to do a short-term trial run with us, because they were Yahoo and didn't want to offer us very much. It was like a six-month deal, and I said, "No way! Six months in internet times is years. We need a buy-out on this."

We went back and forth with them several times until they finally came to terms with us. They got a really good deal, I got out of debt with it, and my partner ended up going to work for them and becoming the Chief of Yahoo Games for seven years before he left. To this date, if you log in to Yahoo Games and sit down at one of the game tables, you can select an avatar that represents you. One of them is a guy with a red cap, glasses and a goatee, and that would be me – only, I shave now! But the avatar has not yet shaved.

Chambers:
Launching that and going into the AdSense world in 2004, what was that like with the e-book? Was that the first product you sold online?

Comm:
It really was the first product that was mine. I really had not entered into the Internet Marketing realm. I didn't know much about copywriting, I didn't know about long-form sales letters, I didn't know

much about shopping carts – most of the commerce I did online was affiliate programs promoting other people's products and services. So, I never had to worry about processing stuff on my own. It was a really neat experience! When you're creating a digital product like an e-book, it's just ones and zeroes. Your overhead is negligible and the instant gratification of the delivery system to the customer is great. They're willing to pay a little bit more than they would for a physical product because they know that they can download it right away, and jump right in. So, to be able to put a 66-page book online for $77 and see it sell like it did was very rewarding.

Chambers:

That is incredible, because when you go over to the store and a book is 200-300 pages, it's for $19. So, with the e-book, you're going over $1.10 per page! What gave you the idea to make the price that high?

Comm:

Well, I looked at what was going on in the e-book marketplace, and I knew that there were very few that were that expensive, but I also knew the value of what we had to offer – my story was completely true and legitimate, and if people would read the book and then develop a website like I say they should, then they had an opportunity to make a lot of money. To this day, I still get testimonials from people who read my material and tell me that it's been very profitable for them. It's all in the value – would you spend $100 to make $1000? Would you spend $1000 to make $10,000? Sure! I'd do that all day long! We had the proof that it was doable and people were willing to give us a chance.

Chambers:

If people want to get hold of that book now, is there a site that they can go to buy it?

Comm:

It's actually kind of funny because four editions later, the book is 230 pages long – it's revised and extended to be current. As of last week, we're doing something that we've never done before… we're giving it away for free. I believe that we've got a lot of success publishing this book; we're in our third year of it, and I really want to get this material to people's hands. If they go to www.adsense-secrets.com, they can find out how they can download a free copy.

Chambers:

What was it like going from an e-book to a hard-copy book, and then having a New York Times bestseller?

Comm:

Well, it was a great experience! I am of the mindset that publishing a book is really not about book sales. As an author, what I discovered was that most authors don't know how to leverage their book to have the type of success that they really desire. They think it's all about how many books they are going to sell. The fact of the matter is that most authors out there today are starving artists – they don't generate the kind of revenue they want because they don't know how to position the book and then, they don't know how to leverage the book to the next thing. They think that the book is the end in itself.

With us, we were never concerned about how many books we sold. Although I know we sold tens of thousands of copies of the AdSense

Code, it was all about branding. You can sell thousands of copies of an e-book at $97, which is where our price had landed with the second edition, and it's impressive to a certain group of people. But, when you have a physical, traditionally created book in your hands, your credibility somehow goes through the roof. We just grant that credibility to people who have a book. It's an authority piece. And so, we knew that the next step was to take this material to the mainstream, to do a traditionally published book. And that book would then give more credibility to me as the expert in the area, and it would act as a lead generation tool.

So, the same material people were paying $97 for, they could get it on www.amazon.com for sale at $16.72 as a physical book. But as a lead generator, we would then build customers that would hopefully become lifetime customers – sending them to a website where they would register their book in order to get additional bonuses. That has been what I did with book and that has been the end result. So, I'm pretty pleased with that.

As far as getting it on the New York Times Bestseller List, we never would have imagined that was going to happen. I actually heard about it from an associate at a different publishing house, who wrote to me and said, "Congratulations on New York Times Bestseller Status!" I said, "What?!" We had made it all the way to Number Three on www.amazon.com, and Number One in all the categories, but I did not know we were going to be able to push it that far. We hit Number Six on the Business Paperback List – I think we were on the list two months running. We also hit the Business Week Bestseller List. So, that was pretty exciting!

Chambers:

I'm sure the readers would love to know how long it took you to get from the Start to the End of the New York Times bestseller... how long did it take until you had a physical copy of the book in hand?

Comm:

I had the book in hand at the end of March or the beginning of April, 2006. I hit the June Bestseller List.

Chambers:

You've got to be very pleased with that!

Comm:

I was! I was thrilled with it! One of the great things about being a New York Times Bestseller is that once you're a New York Times bestseller, you're always a New York Times Bestseller. I'll be 80 years old and still be leveraging that! Hopefully, we'll hit it a few more times before then; but if not, it's still a token that you can wear for the rest of your life.

Chambers:

You are phenomenal at positioning and leveraging your material... help the readers understand what that means.

Comm:

When you've got a physical book, the people in the media take you more seriously. You're not going to get book reviews for an e-book. It's very rare that that happens – you might get reviews on some on-line sites and blogs, but the larger media is not going to pay attention to an e-book. But, they are going to pay attention to a physical book. You're going to get more reviews and radio coverage, you're going to get more television coverage and you're going to get more articles written about you.

As a result, when an organization is looking for a speaker to discuss a certain niche, there could be ten different people out there and maybe nine of them have written e-books, but one of them has written a physical book... who do you think they're going to pick to come be the expert? The guy who's written the physical book, because of the credibility that comes with having this physical item which you can put in your hand and show to people, that you can send in the mail, that can you personalize with an autograph and send as a gift – that just opens new doors. Honestly, for the time and expense involved in creating a book, it's got to be the item with the lowest barrier of entry that brings the greatest potential reward.

Chambers:
As an employer, what does it take to be a good leader?

Comm:
Well, first and foremost, to run a business which is outstanding, I believe that you want to have the highest morals and ethics in everything you do, and you want to be a good example to your employees. I think people have a hard time following those who don't give a sense that 'The most important thing in what we're doing is that we have a great positive outcome for our customers and that we serve them and meet their needs'.

I think if you've got employees that understand that your goal is excellent, then they're going to perform at their very best, and the outcome is going to be exactly that. When there are issues, deal with them quickly, professionally and in the most ethical way possible. You want to inspire people to do the task and have a position that excites them. In other words, don't try to fit square pegs in round holes; find out what people's passions are, and what their gifts and talents and abilities are, and plug them into an area where they can express those gifts and talents in a very positive workplace environment.

Reward them for work well done. It is pure capitalism – the American dream is for every person to be able to do that which they were made to do. And I think when people are doing that, they're just going to be so much more content and happy that work doesn't feel like work anymore; it's play! They're doing it because they want to do it, and it's a bonus that they get paid.

Chambers:

When you're having a tough time in your work as an entrepreneur, what do you do to stay focused?

Comm:

When I am having a tough time, there are a couple of things I like to do. I like to work hard and play hard. The truth of the matter is that when I got into computers, I got into them because I enjoyed playing computer games. As of this interview, I'm 44 years old and I still do!

And so, decompression for me is to sit down, and I might be at the computer, but I'm playing World of Warcraft with my kids... something to take my mind off work. I find that when I don't think too hard about things, my sub-conscious gets to work on them... and if I just wait for the answer, for the right timing, then usually it will just present itself in my mind and I'll know what to do. I don't mind the pressure of the deadlines and having to get things done because I am a 'Type A' personality. But, I don't like to force things either.

We do many things here – if you could see my whiteboard right now with all the projects we've got going on, the odds are that you would say, "You're insane. You're certifiable. You should be locked up and taken away. Nobody can accomplish all that!" The truth is that that might be true, but we're working to shoot high and try to accomplish as much as we can. In the worst case scenario, we say, "Look… let's either not do that project, or let's put it off for the time because we've got all this other cool stuff going on".

There's just so much opportunity today – it's all over the place! The internet offers opportunity unlike any other I've ever seen in my lifetime and I think if we asked our parents and their parents and their parents' parents, they would probably say the same thing, because the barriers for entry for getting online are so low and the opportunity is so great.

Chambers:

How do you define success?

Comm:

I define success as, "If you're living your life in a way that is honoring and ethical, and you're doing good stuff for other people… if you're pouring yourself into helping others' quality of life increase – whether that's by having employees that you can give a job to, and thereby they're blessed and they're able to support their families and pass it on, or whether it's for the customer whose life we can enrich by providing quality information that helps them to be blessed and then reach their goals.

I can't put a monetary description on it because I don't think that's it; I think that if you're doing what you love, the reward is going to follow. Whether that's money, or satisfaction, or contentment... it's always going to come if you're just following that passion and doing what you love to do. To me, that's success.

Chambers:

Are you still very passionate about your work?

Comm:

I am so passionate about my work. I love what I do! I love coming up with new ideas, sitting down with my team – Ken Burge who is the President of our company and was with Microsoft for almost 9 years as a technology evangelist is an absolutely brilliant guy; Dan Nickerson – he's got the title of Vice President of Ideas; Joel Ownby–our content specialist. We sit down in our meetings and brainstorm – we laugh, we have a great time coming up with ideas, we filter through, we decide 'this is what we're going to do'. Everybody's locked and loaded to take up their role in it, and then it's exciting to have a product launched, to see it become successful, celebrate and then move on to the next thing.

There's always a next thing. It's not like I can see an end game in what we do here because there's always something new and creative to come up with.

Chambers:

What new projects are you working on in the niches that you absolutely love?

Comm:

I've been using social media a lot lately – Twitter, Facebook, YouTube, MySpace, StumbleUpon – and I've really discovered how to leverage Web 2.0 sites and social media sites to drive traffic to build community to build my business. I was just asked by a major publisher to do a definitive guide to using Twitter for business. So, we're actually in the midst of that right now. It's called 'Twitter Power' and should be on bookshelves by February '09. They're moving it quickly!

Chambers:

Tell me about 'Click Here to Order'.

Comm:

'Click Here to Order' was actually an interesting project to do. When I was doing the reality show 'The Next Internet Millionaire', I had the opportunity to work with a lot of my peers because we brought them on location, to the set of the show, so they could teach the contestants about how they make money online. The contestants learned everything from copywriting, and viral marketing, to business building and ecommerce and so on.

As I got to know my associates better, I discovered that we're all just regular folks that had stumbled into the opportunity to build a business online. As a result, we became wealthy doing so. And I though, "There are biographies out there on the big boys – like the Google Story, the Yahoo Story and eBay–the Perfect Store, but nobody's really talking about the guys who are making millions of dollars at home, doing business online". So, I set out to interview a lot of these guys – I did about 60 hours of interviews and rather than create a book of interviews with a chapter on each one, we stitched it together as a narrative that tells a story – the History of Internet Marketing, or Information Marketing, if you will, from the very beginning of the internet up through the rise of the e-book and the teleseminar and the webinar and the information product. The book gives the background.

So, it's not so much a 'how to make money online' book, as it is an inspirational story that reveals how these people got started and what obstacles they faced, and what triumphs came as a result. We are pretty excited about it. We had Number 16 on www.amazon.com of all the books in the world, Number 1 across all Business categories, and Number 12 on www.barnesandnoble.com. The book has been very well received and has got five star-reviews across the board, and we're still doing a lot of radio interviews about that, and have plenty of articles coming out.

So when we speak of positioning, this book was written to help get me outside of the box of the AdSense Guy. That was part of the reason why I did the reality show as well – to show people that we're pretty well-rounded in business, especially internet business, and also to provide a platform that would expose internet marketing and those of us who are in that industry to a much wider audience, rather than those who are in the smaller circle that already knows about the industry.

Chambers:

A book is one thing; but to host and create your own television show is a whole another round... what was it like hosting and creating 'The Next Internet Millionaire'?

Comm:

It was actually pretty exciting. I had gone to my partner Eric Holmlund, who I did several successful product launches with. It was in January '07, and I was in the shower–I don't know why, but I always get my best ideas, or even some of my most disastrous ideas, in the shower. I'm a fan of reality television and enjoyed the first couple of seasons of 'The Apprentice' and I enjoyed 'The Amazing Race' and 'Survivor'. I thought, "Video online is popular, as it is. Isn't it time that there were some original quality productions that were done just for the internet?"

I contacted Eric, and he had told me that he wanted to get into video. So, he agreed to do it and we began putting together the pre-production for auditions. We had close to 300 people at the auditions on YouTube. We selected 12 contestants – 6 men and 6 women – from the US, Canada, the UK and Costa Rica, and brought them all on location to Colorado for a two-week intensive. We were going to shoot six days on, one day off and six days on, and get the whole show done in that period of time.

We brought in a dozen internet millionaires – each one on a different day – to teach the contestants. The contestants would learn and then they were put to the test both as teams and as an individual. There were eliminations almost on a daily basis. And by the end, we had one winner – the last standing – who received $25,000 cash and a Joint Venture with me. With the person who won, we did $70,000 in a week in the Joint Venture together. And so, it was successful – it took up almost a whole year by the time we got done with the planning, auditions, shooting the show in July and early August, and then going immediately into post-production and releasing one episode online each week.

People can actually go see the show online if they want to, at www. nextinternetmillionaire.com, or they can go to www.barnesandnoble. com and do a search for the show – the DVD box-set is available with a bunch of extras on it as well – if they choose to watch it on their television. All in all, I'm very pleased with all that, and not a week goes by when someone doesn't ask me when we're going to do Season Two because they want to audition, or they want to cover it. We've moved on to a lot of other things and the only way I would do another season is if we had a major network who loved this idea and this brand, and all we have to do was to go on location and shoot... because I don't want to go through that again!

Chambers:

What advice would you give to a young entrepreneur who wants to get out there and do it?

Comm:

Well firstly, the first thing you've got to do is know what you want to do. A lot of people go at it backwards – they think, "Okay! What can I do, that can make money?" I think that's the wrong way to approach it. I think the right approach is, "What am I passionate about? Where is my training? What do I really want to be when I grow up?" which is a question I constantly ask myself to make sure that I'm doing what I want to do.

I really have a firm belief that, if you're doing what you love, then money and rewards are naturally going to follow. So, pursue that – learn all you can about your particular passion and niche. Connect with other people in the industry. Find those that you can serve – how can you help other people? I guarantee that when you can help other people to achieve their goals and reach what they're going for, then it's going to come back around. When you're doing good stuff, then good stuff is going to happen. Pursue it relentlessly – don't listen to the voices that tell you that you're not good enough, or that you can't do it, or who do you think you are, because the greatest success stories are those who persist beyond that.

Chambers:

What is the greatest risk that you have ever taken and was it worth it?

Comm:

I think the greatest risk I've ever taken is that right now, over the past couple of years, I've basically staffed up from two people to fifteen. It costs a lot of money to create an office environment and everything that goes along with that, and pay the salaries, and offer benefits. I'm really investing a lot of my money into the belief that, if I stayed small and did it on my own, I could make a couple of million dollars a year and speak a little bit and have fun, but never get beyond that.

What I want to do is build companies that get sold for 8 or 9 figures and in doing so, have a very positive impact on my employees, on my customers, and then be able to take net proceeds from that and have a greater impact in the world. So, right now, I suppose, is my greatest risk.

Chambers:

What type of a legacy do you want to leave?

Comm:

I'd like my tombstone to say three words – 'He got it'. Not necessarily even, 'He did it', because we all do it, one way or another, and some-times what we do isn't good; but to say that I got to the end of the road and that it was my reason and my purpose for being here that I latched on to, made a difference... 'He got it'.

For more information, visit:

www.joelcomm.com

Chapter 3

Bill Hoffer

Image and Wardrobe Consultant

David E. Chambers (Chambers):

In your experience dealing with executives and high profile people, as a wardrobe consultant and your Chamber of Commerce work, what does it take to be a leader?

Bill Hoffer (Hoffer):

There are so many things that make the answer to that question different for different types of professions or associations. Generally speaking, with my business in mind, I believe that great leaders are great readers. I've always remembered that phrase. In addition, you

42

must always be growing. A leader has to be a great example. He or she has to have the ability to connect with all types of personalities and to inspire other people by example. A leader needs to possess consistency, dependability, and trustworthiness.

Communication, also, is so critical in any relationship, but especially in business and in leadership roles. Being sincere and genuine without being manipulative, having the best interests of others at heart so that they can maximize their potential, and stepping outside the box in terms of creativity and thinking are important. So is knowing and understanding the law of attraction, and the law of importance. A leader must also realize that people need to feel appreciated and want to have a sense of belonging.

Chambers:

Are leaders born, or are leaders developed?

Hoffer:

I think they can be developed. With some leaders it may simply be a natural talent or a certain personality profile. You learn a lot about personalities in my business and in sales in general. The different types of primary and secondary personality combinations can determine whether or not an individual has the ability to become a leader, but I don't think one is born a leader. I think ultimately, leaders are people who have the ability to grow, learn, and be mentored in leadership.

Chambers:

You have one of the most successful clothing companies in Seattle, Washington. You've also done business in Texas. With your clientele and the leaders you've worked with, what are three traits that stand out in your mind as true leadership?

Hoffer:

Inspiration, example, integrity are true principles in business.

Chambers:

How do you define success?

Hoffer:

For me, it's the number of people in life that you have a positive impact on. It's not about your bank account or tangible assets. It's not the title after your name that matters.

I've always felt that the number of people who show up for someone's funeral is a great way to measure their success, or their legacy. The only problem with that concept is that you may outlive the majority of them. So it may not be as accurate of a gauge as one might wish. There are certain principles of life that you find in all great success stories. There's no room for ego in the word success. It's in the eyes of others to observe, and not for you to advertise or brag about. Success means always reaching out to help others that are less fortunate, and to pay it forward without any expectation or agenda.

Chambers:

You deal with a lot of very influential and highly successful people, and I know that relationships are key to the success of your business. How have you kindled relationships with high-profile people?

Hoffer:

By being sincere and genuine, by having a lot of self-confidence and ability, and by just taking small successes in your life and reflecting back on them as proof that whatever you focus on, you get. If you think positively, you'll act positively, and you'll attract positive energy. If you're always in the dump and feeling sorry for yourself, you are not going to be very attractive to anybody. They are not going to want to be around you.

I had a friend that I went to college with, someone I'd known for about fifteen years in Houston, and at that time I was not very mature in understanding relationships, or life. But, little by little, as I grew I began to realize what my relationship with him was really all about. It was about what he could get out of it, and not about what he could give to it. I'd lost contact with him, and one day, out of the blue, he called me and he wanted to get together and talk.

He'd had a lot of personal problems over the years. He was just a mess. I knew that as long as I had him in my life he was not going to be a positive influence, and I just told him I couldn't be his friend anymore. It was a real breakthrough for me because I had never done that. I'd never actually told someone that I just couldn't have them in my life any longer. I told him that our relationship wasn't a positive influence for me, that it was holding me back. I told him that until he could change, I couldn't help him.

I believe that relationships are about being a giver, not a taker. They're about setting a great example, and just being totally genuine and sincere..........being real.

Chambers:

Bill, you touched on one of the secrets to success that most people don't realize, which is: sometimes you have to eliminate certain relationships in business, and in life. How do you go about doing that, and do you believe that it's a part of succeeding?

Hoffer:

It's definitely part of succeeding; it's a decision. Success is an accumulation of a lot of decisions in life. Relationship decisions are also an element of maturity as well as part of the maturation process. It's an evolution of you as an individual to understand and make the connection about how important those decisions are. Sometimes they are very, very tough ones.

In terms of relationships, I've had a nasty divorce; a lot of people don't have to go through that. I didn't think that I would ever have to go through it, but that was ten years ago and that was a life changing event for me. It kind of set me on my path to where I am today by helping me to understand the value of making tough decisions.

Sometimes, it may appear on the surface that you are being selfish, but the decision is appropriate because you have a goal. You have a vision of who you are, what you want to be, and a direction you want to head in. No matter how vague it might be, it still should be overriding enough to permit you be honest with clients who are not treating the relationship in a professional, respectful manner. It's the same for friends who are impeding your progress toward your personal or business goals.

I've been engaged in many areas, such as coaching, studying real estate investing, business, and volunteer work with the Chamber of Commerce. I have so many things on my plate that I really don't have time for personal relationships with people who are not a joy to be around, or who don't have a lot of positive stuff going on that I can feed off of and lend them support. You just have to surround yourself with like minded, successful, high energy people. That's what I focus on right now when I meet people: "Is this someone I really want to get to know, and why?"

Chambers:

What is the recipe for finding success in your line of work?

Hoffer:

In my line of work, it's a combination of a lot of things. For instance, I've seen a lot of good salesmen over the years in my business. In fact, there is one in particular who stands out whom I worked with in Dallas.

When I joined the company in 1989, he was a leader. He had an office of his own, though he was probably only about thirty-years-old at the time. He was very charismatic and dynamic; one of those guys who like to be the center of attention, and generally was. He could go to a client's house and lay out a $50,000 wardrobe and he could ask the guy to buy it all. On several occasions, they did. But he could not run a business. He was not detail oriented; he was just a great salesman.

In my business, you have to not only be a good salesperson, with honesty and integrity, but you have to be able to handle the details, have structure, and consistency in your work ethic. You set certain times that you do specific things, and you have to be diligent in doing those every day. This business is all about prospecting and asking for an appointment, getting the appointment and making a solid presentation, asking for the order then delivering the order. It's about making the customer happy.

I've always had the attitude that if someone bought from me the first time, he was only going to buy from me again if I performed. The second time he bought, he wanted to confirm that what happened the first time was actually going to happen again. The third time he bought from me, then I knew that he was actually a client.

I've had many, many, many times when a prospect would tell me, "Boy you sure are persistent." To me that's a compliment, because I have a lot of confidence in what I do. I know that when I get an opportunity to work with someone, they will not be disappointed. There is always that exception; that one guy who has such high expectations that there is no way in the world you're going to be able to meet them. These type's have what we call caviar taste buds and a Budweiser pocketbook. I think I've only had clients like that a handful of times over the last nineteen years.

Chambers:

What inspired you to get into your industry?

Hoffer:

Quite frankly, when I got into my industry I was on the back end of having spent about sixteen months looking for my next opportunity. I'd spent the previous twelve years with a pharmaceutical company. I wasn't sure what I was going to find, going forward.

I always tell the story from the standpoint that it was divine intervention. I met a stranger in a church I'd never attended before. We had a brief conversation, he gave me his business card and he asked me to come talk to him that week. Two weeks later he hired me. He was one of the best mentors and personal examples of a Christian who did not try to preach or convert me, but who just lived his life as an example. He personally had a lot to do with what inspired me to stay in this business.

Chambers:

After you were in the business, when was that point where you knew you loved what you did?

Hoffer:

Probably after about a year or two. By then I'd developed the knowledge and expertise necessary to give me enough confidence that I could sit in front of people who made more money than I did and give them a presentation. When I knew I could call a complete stranger on the phone, after I'd sent a mailer to them, and ask for an appt. (Before the days of e-mail our first contact with people was through a postal mailer, and then we followed up with a phone call.) I had to develop the confidence to know that, *Hey, this gentleman needs to give me an appointment because I have something really important that will be beneficial to him.*

I really began to love my profession when I realized I was working with successful people, and I wanted to be just like them. So, little by little, and step by step, I built my business in Dallas, until 1993 when I had a one-on-one with the CEO of the company. He lived in the Dallas area, so I had more access to him than I would have if I had lived in another city. I'd been with the company for almost five years. That day, he asked me if I would be interested in having an office of my own. I'd never thought about doing that. I was honored and flattered that he would even ask me.

The company had over a hundred offices around the country at that time. They didn't ask me to open an office in Seattle specifically, but the end result of that conversation was to do my research and determine where I would like to open up a new one. I looked in INC, Money and some other magazines which listed the top twenty best places to live in the United States. Seattle kind of stood out above all the rest. I had traveled there when I was in the pharmaceutical industry as a Division Manager. I put together a business plan and made a couple of trips to Seattle to check out the market for office space and living accommodations. The company accepted my plan, and I moved out here in March of 1994. I remember the first day I walked into the office. There was carpet; there were walls and windows—but no furniture, no computers, no fax machine, no phones, and no clients.

Chambers:

You've mentioned self confidence a couple of times. To open an office by yourself, and to be inspired to really go for it, where did you derive your self-confidence to be the success you are today?

Hoffer:

I'd accomplished a lot in the years leading up to that particular point. The great success of life, the end result, is the legacy that you leave. We never stop growing. Everyday is part of our growth process, with small successes leading to greater successes.

I think that the experience of flunking out of college and working for three years in the real world, made me realize that I wasn't going to get very far if I didn't finish my degree. I went back and basically had to have a 4.0 for the remaining thirty-six credit hours in order to raise my grade point average enough to be able to walk across the stage and accept my diploma. At that point in my life, that was a

HUGE accomplishment.

There was a time in my life when I took some coaching and one of the processes that was involved was an exercise that was called "Your Bullet Bio." What you do in this exercise is go back as far as you can remember to events in your past. It doesn't have to be defined by positive or negative, it just needs to be a thought, experience, person, event or moment. You take a piece of paper and draw lines across the page, about a half-inch apart. Then you draw a line down the middle, and you have anywhere from forty to fifty separate lines. On each one of those you just put a statement, comment, name or thought. At the end of the exercise, I had thirteen pages. I thought to myself, "Man........I just wrote a book. I have an outline for a book about my life story!"

In all of that were reminders to me of my accomplishments. There were an incredible amount of success stories in there that I'd forgotten about. When you add them all up, you realize that you were feeding off each individual success, by just knowing that you had the ability. I was national salesman of the year for my pharmaceutical company. There were probably a couple of hundred people in a sales position with them nationally. Later, I was in the "President's Club" in the clothing company, the top tier of sales people selling at about a half-million dollars and above for a year. This was before I went out on my own to have my current business. I was on the honor roll in high school. I never really achieved in much in sports because I wore glasses and I couldn't play football, and wasn't good enough in baseball. However, I was good in bowling, so there was a sport that I did excel in.

Where I get my self-confidence is kind of in a subconscious sort of way, because I am not the type of person that brags about himself. I don't have a big ego or go around talking about myself. In fact I tend to ask a lot of questions. The reason I'm successful in sales is that I ask questions and I listen rather than trying to convince others how great I am.

Chambers:

So by listing the Bullet Bio were you able to see the successes through-out your life which became the source of your confidence?

Hoffer:

Yes. I think it was primarily a state of mind. I'd had great mentors too, and part of what I learned by doing the Bullet Bio was where my mentors were in my life story.

I also got a perspective on my decision-making. I discovered that most of the bad decisions I had made were in my personal life. I had made great decisions in my business life. After doing the exercise and seeing this insight, my decision-making in my personal life has gotten better.

Chambers:

How have coaches and mentors helped you become more successful?

Hoffer:

I think that's the critical part of success: getting coaching and mentor-ing. Even Tiger Woods, literally the greatest golfer on the planet, has a coach. Successful businessmen who are multi-millionaires have coaches. It's part of the learning process, too. Never stop growing. We talked about principles of life and business earlier, in terms of *what does it take to be successful*, and I think it includes understanding that the process is one of continual growth. For me personally, I want to get something new out of each and every day.

Chambers:

How does one go about finding a great mentor or great coach?

Hoffer:

Mentors and coaches have to be willing to connect with you when you reach out to them. But, first of all, you have to make the decision that you want a coach.

In the beginning, I didn't realize that I had mentors. I didn't see them as mentors, but that's who they were. Timing is everything in life, and you have to recognize that person as being someone who can help you. Then you have to ask them for their help. You look for people who you can connect with and who have no agenda—people who are givers, not takers.

I have been a mentor myself. For about four years now, I've been a mentor with the Graduate School of Business at Seattle University. Back in 1996-98, I also worked on an advisory board for Big Brothers here in King County. Being affiliated with both organizations showed that I had a passion for helping people. I believe I am also a mentor for my clients. I think I teach them a lot about clothing, image, fashion, first impressions, and how that all ties in with what their goals are in life.

My point is that a mentor need not be a professional coach. Your mentor may be a company executive, an administrator in a non-profit organization, a friend, etc. Principally, they are people who have life experiences which they share, and in doing so, they shorten the runway for you.

Chambers:

What was your greatest "Ah ha" moment in business?

Hoffer:

It happened when I was working in the hospital, after I'd flunked out of college. After three years of being a purchasing agent there, it became apparent to me that without finishing college, I wasn't going to have the opportunity to reach my full potential. I realized that a lot of doors would remain closed to me without that degree.

Getting the degree didn't actually make me any *smarter*. I can tell you that I don't recall any of the courses that I took in college as having a direct impact on where I am today. Like a boot camp in the military, it was a testing stage in life that showed I had what it takes to move on to the next level. Of course we've all heard of people who've achieved great things without having a college degree, but for me, that was the "Ah ha" moment in my own life. I didn't yet know about entrepreneurship; I believed that a degree was going be critical for me to succeed. I was always taught, "Get your college degree and get a job."

As it turned out, after I'd gone back and finished the degree, everything changed. I then had the ability to get a job as a corporate purchasing agent for a healthcare provider before moving on to sales. I don't think I would have been on the path to where I am today without that degree. It proved I could set a goal and achieve it.

Chambers:

What strategies for time management do you use?

Hoffer:

First of all, you need to have your long and short term goals clearly defined. Otherwise you are just fooling yourself with your time management. It's useful to review those goals periodically because they do change. I do that at least once every year, usually at the end of the year. Once you have your goals clearly defined, you look at the reasons why you want to achieve those goals. Then you put together a plan, work the plan, and incorporate a time table so that you have the ability to measure your progress. You break it down into the daily steps necessary to lead you to achieving that goal. You perform those activities on a consistent basis. It takes a combination of personal discipline and structure. The reason most people fail in business is that they don't have the discipline, and they haven't formed the habits that allow them to succeed.

I received a pamphlet when I got into the clothing business which I still keep with me today. It was a shortened version of a book which was written by a really successful insurance salesman named Albert Gray in the 1950s. It's called *The Common Denominator of Success*. Everybody is always looking for the magic formula, the silver bullet; the single answer to "What does it take to be successful?" It is so simple, but yet a lot of people won't buy into it. The secret of success is forming the habits of doing the things that failures don't want to do.

Chambers:

For my final question I'd like to ask, what advice would you give to a budding entrepreneur?

Hoffer:

My advice is for them to find a mentor or coach who can hold them accountable to their goals. New entrepreneurs must set some short-term goals that are realistic and achievable, so that they can gain some level of self-confidence—which is a huge factor in success.

That person needs to be passionate about what they are doing, and be honest with themself. They must not take shortcuts. They need to maintain integrity and be willing to let go of people who try to discourage them or steal their dreams.

I would advise them to read books, especially on the power of thought. The power of a person's thoughts can't be overstated. Some key books essential to a personal library include: *Think and Grow Rich*, *As a Man Thinketh*, and The *Greatest Salesman In The World*. These are a few examples of books any successful person already knows about.

I also think that developing affirmations to feed your mind with messages of positive encouragement on a daily basis is essential. Be grateful for what you have and never give up.

Chambers:

That was a beautiful way to end. Is there anything else you would like to add?

Hoffer:

A lot of people ask me from time to time why I do what I do. I never had any idea that I would be in the clothing business before I got into this industry. Moreover, I never had any idea that I would have my own business, and have total control of my life. Because of fate or destiny, or perhaps just the natural process of choice, here I am today. I love the feeling that I get when I put a garment on someone for the first time and watch how it makes them feel like a million bucks.

The friendships and relationships that I have are the best part of what I do. I have a network of friends and clients who are there to help me in their area of expertise, if I need them. I work with a lot of attorneys, financial and real estate people, CEOs, health care providers, and architects. It's a great feeling when they share with me the compliments that they get while wearing my product. I just talked with a client last week who'd had dinner with two of my other clients—these are people who were referrals from another client. They were all at the same table having dinner, and I was the topic of conversation because they were all wearing my suits, and my shirts. What a great referral network......

Chambers:

Bill, I can't thank you enough for being part of this book. There is no one else I would rather have built me a custom uniform, which is how I always think of it. In the military you have a uniform. In business you have a uniform. As a CEO you have a uniform, and when you put that on, you feel different. You know you are different because of it. I can't thank you enough.

Bill Hoffer
Wardrobe Design

Seattle, Wa. 98109
206-571-6687

Bill@WardrobeDesign.net
b.hoffer@comcast.net
www.wardrobedesign.net

Chapter 4

Chuck Kammer

Business Strategist and Consultant

David E. Chambers (Chambers)

You run a few multimillion dollar businesses. How did you get into what you do now?

Chuck Kammer (Kammer):

My father was in the automotive business, on the mechanic side of it, and when I came to California I was introduced to it through a friend at Walnut Valley Auto Body. I started at the very bottom sweeping floors, moving cars around, etc. I learned a lot about the business real quick.

Chambers:

You have a very interesting story of starting from nothing and work-ing your way up. How long did it take you to get to the point where you owned your own shops?

Kammer:

From the time I started sweeping floors to owning my own shop, it took twelve years.

Chambers:

That's a long time to be passionate about one thing, and keep going. How did you stay focused, and what kept that drive going?

Kammer:

Just knowing that I could do it. I think I took my time a little bit. I would say the last three years of that was just total procrastination— just waiting to take the jump. I knew that when I did it, I wanted to be the best. I wanted to do it right, so I actually bounced around from job to job in order to learn the things I felt I needed to learn from dealerships, independents, and corporate owned body shops, so that I could see the industry from all angles.

Chambers:

With your company, Kammer Management you go in and consult with other companies. Going back to what you said about taking that leap, how do you coach or instruct people to take the leap, and really go for their passions and dreams?

Kammer:

I don't think anyone ever reaches their true potential in life, because we all have doubts and fear. The most successful people have found away to minimize or work around doubt. Strong passion, confidence, faith and especially knowledge will really do a number on doubt and fear. If you're passionate about something you will get good at it. I like to point out their past accomplishments, skills and qualities. Go over their numbers work with them to help them shed the doubt. So they have the knowledge and feel good about taking the leap.

Chambers:

So does it come down to relying on what you know in terms of having that confidence and that knowledge within?

Kammer:

Absolutely.

Chambers:

It sounds like when you counsel other shops, and for yourself when you went out on your own, it comes down to finding that confidence from within. How does someone do that?

Kammer:

I think the human tendency is to look at the mistakes we've made in our own lives. Usually you have someone who is a successful manager, or you have someone who just has a dream. They tend to look at the negatives, when in fact, they should look at the accomplishments that they've made—whether those successes were claimed by the company they worked for, or whether it's a personal obstacle that they overcame such as a bad divorce, or business decision.

I think getting to know them, and reminding them of what they are made of, what they can do when they are on top of their game, and helping them find what they love and are passionate about helps them gain the momentum and frame of mind that they need. Henry Ford said, *"If you think you can, you can. If you think you can't, you're right."* I believe that 100%, and I just don't think that the confidence to go out and buy or create a big company like Microsoft is going to happen overnight. I think you have to take stock of the accomplishments you've made, and build up to something like that.

Chambers:

Most people get stuck in fear. They're going forward in the right direction, and then they hit this element of fear which they must break through in order to have success. Most people stop when they hit that fear. What advice do you give someone to help them move beyond fear, and eliminate the roadblocks to success?

Kammer:

I get as much information as I can, and try to help them change their thought process. When I was growing up and expressed my dreams the people close to me would, point out obstacles instead of giving encouragement.

Often times when I say things like, "You need to call in a supplement for additional funds if needed and you don't have a contract with that insurance company or don't call one in if you do have a contract and you supplement rate is too high" The clients usually respond with a fear driven excuse, ". I can't afford to pay people to do that." Or I need to be paid on every little thing I do to a car! Contract or not! I'll show them numbers from the shops I have managed, or the one I have now, and show them what the positive effects are.

Chambers:

To overcome your fear, it seems that it's crucial to understand as many elements of the industry as possible. I know that you are very good with the numbers, and understand them. How has knowing the numbers of your business helped you succeed?

Kammer:

It's just like driving a race car, especially if you're pushing it to its limit. You look at your gauges. In business, the numbers are your gauges. If you are running hot, you know you maybe running lean; revving too high or your air flow is restricted or maybe something else needs attention. In looking at a client's numbers myself, I wouldn't recommend them to grow or to move forward until they had all their gauges in place, so that they were ready to accelerate—to push it to the very maximum. Showing them their numbers and showing their history, I can demonstrate to them that the numbers will tell them when to hit the gas, and when to brake. For instance, sometimes having too much work can actually be a problem. It can drastically slow production and drain the bank account if you're buying tons of parts—so you have to know your numbers. In a case like that if your account is getting low because you've spent a bunch of money on payroll and parts for cars which aren't completed, it's like running out of oil.

So having the gauges in place and tracking your numbers makes a huge difference. It helps show you what your next move should be, or what needs your attention.

I have an associate who I can't counsel, because he's my competitor, but as my friend we talk occasionally. I ask him, "How are your numbers?" and he says he doesn't know. If there's money to spend on a new dirt bike he takes the money out. I ask, "Do you know what your indirect or direct expenses are? How about your gross profit or your net profit, or which account is making you the most money and which one isn't? Do you know how your overtime is affecting your bottom line?" He doesn't know. He's got a shop that is a little bit smaller than mine, and he never has any money. It's because he's not looking at his gauges. He can't win the race if he really doesn't know the perfect time to shift gears. Or if he's running out of fuel too quickly... you get the idea. Knowing your numbers is how you can overcome your fear, and win the race. Knowlege is power.

Chambers:

With Kammer Management. I know you go into a lot of companies, turn them around, and make them more successful by mentoring them. How important is mentorship?

Kammer:

Nothing in this world can change without growth. You have to have a goal. You have to have something that you aspire to. You have to have something that you want to reach for—a carrot, if you will. Someone who is in the same line of work who has succeeded—that's your light at the end of the tunnel. You have to have that light.

Chambers:

When someone is looking for a mentor, what should they look for?

Kammer:

First and foremost, you have to pick a mentor who is honest, and does things with integrity. Pick someone who is loved by many, who has a charitable heart and who is successful in the things that are important to you.

Chambers:

For those who are becoming mentors right now and doing a lot of consulting, what are the best traits for them to have to successfully mentor others?

Kammer:

They need to be extremely positive. Whenever they see an opportunity for improvement, it shouldn't be presented to the owner of the business as a problem.

If I come into a shop and say, "Holy cow! It smells like grease in here," well, that's not the way to do it. The owner loves that place. He goes there every day. He doesn't smell it because he's used to it. Instead of telling him it smells like grease, I'll ask, "How do you think people feel when they come in here? How does it look? How does it smell?" The guy may think its fine, or he might have noticed it himself. In either case, there is a great opportunity. Can you imagine if you go into a fish restaurant, and it reeks of rotten fish? Are you going to want to sit down and eat? It's the same sort of thing. The mentor needs to be optimistic so the person they are mentoring stays open to change.

Chambers:

What does it take to be a great leader?

Kammer:

First off, you have to have a goal. If you look through history and look at any great leader, you'll see someone who had a passionate belief in his or her goal.

It also takes people skills. You have to *like* people to be a great leader. There is something good in everyone, and you have to search for it. A good leader finds out who he or she is leading, and learns about their goals. A good leader may even need to serve those he leads, in order to help them reach their own personal goals. These are the things that inspire someone to want to follow you.

Chambers

How do you define success?

Kammer:

Success is when you experience and live an accomplished goal. Being happy, too, because one person's success could be another person's nightmare. It's very important to know what you want in life, and work toward it. If you don't, you won't ever feel successful.

Chambers:

When times are tough, how do you stay focused?

Kammer:

When times are tough I find the cause and cure, and focus on the cure many times it involves working harder—and smarter. I look at the positive. There are always positive things in every challenge or event.

I started flying. I go to Orange County every once in a while. I used to think, "Man, it's so far away." I realized when I started flying that it's just over the hill; not a big deal. It's all about attitude. It's also changing your perspective. I might be so focused on a problem during the week, but then when I fly over the shop on Saturday, I look down at the building and think, "There is no problem *that* big in that shop down there." Stepping back from a problem and getting perspective on it makes all the difference.

Chambers

What inspired you to get into your line of work?

Kammer:

I love cars. On the mechanic side, usually you are just repairing things. Every once in a while you get the opportunity to do something creative, as far as performance goes. When I was first introduced to collision repair, I remember going into this state of the art facility and seeing cars where half the car body was completely gone. The technicians were so meticulous—they could do anything to a car. A good collision repair facility can do *absolutely anything* to a car. I had the goal of building a vehicle from scratch, and if I'd worked selling cars or as a mechanic, I would never have learned the skills to construct a viable vehicle. That's what inspired me to get into collision repair.

Chambers:

What do most people not know about your industry?

Kammer:

Most people don't realize what I just mentioned; that we can actually do *anything* to any car. It's just a matter of what the car is worth. If a car's not worth that amount of work, then it's time to get another car. I think most people don't know we do mechanical, welding, everything. It's actually a great industry—if you are really good at it—to make a lot of money.

I remember as a kid, I didn't know what I wanted to be. My dad would ask me, "What do you want to be when you grow up?" I would answer, "A millionaire." When he asked how I was going to do that, I would tell him that I didn't know yet. He told me I needed to figure that out. I never in a million years thought it would be in a body shop. I don't think many people really know that you can do so well with a body shop.

Chambers:

What was your biggest "Ah-ha" moment in business?

Kammer:

When I realized that the body shop I'd been managing for nine months was putting $75,000 a month in the bank. I thought, "Holy crap! I've been making this place *that* kind of money?" Then I thought about how much I was earning in comparison. That's when I realized I was ready to go out on my own.

Chambers:

Did you ever run into a situation in which people didn't believe in you?

Kammer:

I think we all do. I had a situation when I was looking at businesses to buy—we were actually in escrow—and the owner of the business asked me, "Why do you want to buy this place, its killing' me?" At the time it was averaging about $26,000 a month in *gross* sales. I said, "This shop could easily do $200,000 on a regular basis, with up to 20% net profit." He had a lot of choice words for me, and warned me that it would never happen, and that I'd better not sue him because, "That's a pipe dream." After three months we were doing $150,000, and after nine months we were up to 200,000. We average about $240,000 a month now. I've had the place for four years.

Chambers:

What time management strategies do you use?

Kammer:

I look at the things that affect other people first. For example, if I have something on the production list that other people are relying on, I put it at the top of my list so that they can stay motivated. If there's a phone call that I need to make to get the ball rolling on something, that's a top priority to me. If I need to talk to my manager about having a team meeting, while I'm in a separate meeting, I do that first. At the bottom of my list are things that need to be done that don't affect as many people or influence production.

Chambers:

What advice or encouragement would you give to a young entrepreneur?

Kammer:

Find something that you really, really love, and are passionate about. Focus on how you think things should be and fill the gap with your actions. In the field or hobby that you love, imagine it like something in the movies, and see what you can accomplish with it.

Chambers:

What inspires you?

Kammer:

People who are extremely motivated. People who had a giant dream and accomplished it. Nice things inspire me. Happy people inspire me. Success stories are a huge inspiration to me.

Chambers:

What do you like best about what you do?

Kammer:

Every day is different. Some days, if I feel like the business needs a little bit of marketing, I do that. I love to solve problems, and there are always a lot of opportunities for that in the automotive and body shop business. And, I still love cars.

Chambers:

What is the greatest risk you've have ever taken, and was it worth it?

Kammer:

Quitting my job and owning my own business was the biggest risk. It was absolutely worth it.

Chambers:

What type of legacy do you want to leave?

Kammer:

I would love to be known as someone who helped others in times of need; someone who inspired others to reach their ultimate goals and realize the most fulfilling lives possible.

Chuck Kammer
Owner and founder of

Collision Center of Temecula, Temecula CA
(951) 695-1233
www.CollisionCenterOfTemecula.com

Kammer Management Inc., Temecula CA
(951) 775-3971

ATS Auto Transport Service, Temecula CA
(951) 252-4396
www.ATS-AutoTransportService.com

Exclusive Autowerks, Temecula CA
(951) 808-3443
www.ExclusiveAutowerks.com

CK Salon, Murrieta CA
(951) 775-2740

Chapter 5

Grace Stephens
Real Estate Investor/Coach

David E. Chambers (Chambers):
Grace, you have an amazing story from being a homeless person to be-
ing a real estate investor. First of all, how did you become homeless and
what transpired from being homeless to becoming an investor?

Grace Stephens (Stephens):
When I graduated from college, my mother was blind in one eye and
had cataract on her other eye. I came home to take care of her and
ended up staying there for 10 years. And by the end of the 10 years, I
suffered from depression and I was really in a very bad place. After

getting into an argument with my mother I moved out of her house. And just took off and drove until I stopped, which happened to be in Santa Barbara. And I found the Salvation Army homeless shelter and got a place to stay and a place to recover. And at that time, I found a temporary job at Delco electronics. While working this temporary job I slept in my car. At the plant they happened to have showers in each of the building, so I slept in my car, took a shower and did everything in the building and so I had that temporary job for 18 months. And there were about 5 of us that worked, some of the engineers, they were also temporary, they didn't want to pay for housing also would stay in their car, so there were about 5 or 6 of us, all wind up on the curb.

Chambers:
How did you get to this amazing state, how did you go from being homeless to investing in real estate?

Stephens:
So there was quite a gap from 1990 until 1992 because I was homeless, my car broke down and I didn't have any, absolutely no where to stay and I got into an argument with one of the ladies at the homeless shelter I was staying at. So I left, and I was sitting on a bench, a park bench at 2 o' clock in the morning with two quarters in my wallet and thinking, you know, where can I go. So I had 3 choices – I could call my dad, or I could call my uncle that lived in Riverside CA, or I could call my mother, who lived in Oregon. So of the three, my dad was the closest but I hadn't seen him in more than 10 years. But I had no other choice, so I called him, and he almost didn't recognize who I was. So he let me come and stay with him and helped me out with my finances, helped me straighten out some things and helped

me get back on my feet. I started working through a temp agency at UCLA. When I was younger I had gone to a real estate seminar and I knew that real estate investing would be the way that I would make money. That it is the best way to get rich. And so that was in 1980s when I first started going to real estate investing seminars, so I came across one in 2005 that seemed to be a combination of all other real estate investing seminars I had gone to previously and they included all the various investing strategies and from them I learned the best combination of requirements for the investing strategy and the type of personality you need in order to succeed at that strategy. And so I have started investing in real estate and I help other people learn how to invest in real estate and become wealthy.

Chambers:

Now that you have gotten into real estate investing, how did it free up your life?

Stephens:

Well, I get to live on a 10-acre ranch site that I have always wanted to live on. Ever since I was 10 years old, we went to Florida to visit my mom's relatives, her brothers, and one of her brothers lived on a 10-acre farm in Central Florida. I have always thought about that, farming, it was beautiful. I always thought that I would like to live on a place like that, so I am able to do that now. I can work from home, I don't have to have set hours, I could choose when I work, I get to drive the car I want, I get to fly in my airplane, I own my own airplane, and I can compete in the regional aerobatic competitions.

You have been able to come from the deepest depths to being very successful now. What advice would you give to someone who is going through a tough time?

Stephens:

Looking for self esteem and motivational classes and start working on yourself, start looking for that little voice in the back of your head that keeps you down, that tells you you are not successful and that nothing is going to work and you know all that stuff in the back of your head, and find a really good competent coach or somebody that you trust that can help you rid yourself of your old tape that will free you to fly, succeed and find whatever it is that makes you happy like when I could afford it, when I had regular money, I would like to go flying because when I fly it makes me happy, you know, when I am up in the air, I forget everything in my life, you know, it is like meditation. So find something that you enjoy that when you are doing it, your mind is free, everything else is not there anymore. That is the same thing that an alcoholic does when they drink, they drink because they want to forget their problems. You don't want to drink, you want to find something that is going to give you peace and joy temporarily so that you can regroup and start over.

Chambers:

How do you define success?

Stephens:

Success to me so far is setting a goal and reaching a goal, the one particularly that I think that I can't, that I won't be able to reach, like learning to fly and getting my college degree, because almost every time I enrolled in my classes I had this nagging doubts that I am not going to be able to do college level work. But I took a class, when I was in the military overseas. One of the semesters, the only class available that I could take was philosophy and philosophy is so un-defined, at least to me it is, that I thought there is no way in the world that I would ever be able to pass a philosophy class but it was the only one, so I enrolled. And I ended up getting a B in that class. And from that time on, I always use that whenever that nagging doubt came on, you know, I passed, so I can probably pass these other classes.

Chambers:

What inspired you to get into real estate investing?

Stephens:

I saw the leverage, you know, buying property at one price and hav-ing it to go up and appreciate its value and when I started taking the real estate investing classes and learning how to buy property below real market, you know, to sell at a higher market, the whole entire dynamics just made sense to me.

Chambers:

Why do you think people are afraid to get into real estate investing?

Stephens:

Because they listen to the media and all the doom and gloom that the media puts out there and they don't understand the dynamics of real estate, they are just afraid, fear. They are afraid of losing money. They just don't find it appealing.

Chambers:

You have obviously overcome a lot of fear in your life, what do you do when you are faced with fear?

Stephens:

I usually just push through and move ahead. Well, I just take a deep breath and go for it.

Chambers:

As you have overcome a lot of fear in your life, as you have gone through ups and downs, you have also mentioned that you had coaching and mentorship, when somebody is looking for a mentor, what should they look for in a mentor?

Stephens:

I think the most important thing in a mentor is someone who knows how to teach because there is a difference between having knowledge and having the ability to impart that knowledge to another person. I have had a lot of teachers that were extremely knowledgeable, they knew their subject inside and out but they could not remember what it was like not knowing. And so they talked way above our heads or they got upset because we could not understand. And so the next most important characteristic is patience.

Chambers:

Ok. Looking back on your successful career, what is that one situation that stood out there that really changed your business? Let me ask the question again, looking back on your success of your business, what is one experience that stood out as a remarkable experience that changed the way you did your business?

Stephens:

Going to a seminar 'that teaches you how you relate to money' because from the time you are young, your attitude, your parents and your siblings and your community are imprinting and pressing on you an attitude towards money, either its scarcity or its abundance or you have to pinch pennies and look at the price of everything you buy and always buy the cheapest thing or you know, you can spend whatever you want and always put it on a credit card and don't worry about it, you know, you grow up with those philosophies, and some of them hold you back, you know, if you have a philosophy that you don't deserve money or rich people are greedy ogres. Then whenever you earn money your subconscious is going influence your decisions on your spending habits which will cause you to lose your money. It is important to learn how to earn and control your money so it doesn't control you.

Chambers:

You mentioned how much education has helped you to overcome your challenges. When someone has those issues with money, where should they turn to, what should they read to help them rewrite their story?

Stephens:

One of the best books is by T Harv Eker called *Secrets Of The Millionaire Mind*, and he goes specifically into, what he calls your money blueprint. And he goes into all those things about how your attitude towards money is imprinted on you very early in age. And the other book that I find very helpful is Jack Canfield's, *The Success Principles*. I think those two are very remarkable books.

Chambers:

As you go through your busy day and you are challenged with all the different properties you own, properties you are buying and people you are coaching, how do you manage your time?

Stephens:

I use a paper daily reminder. I started at an age when paper and pencil were more important than the electronics, so I can't get used to the electronics, so I just use a paper. And I use a 'To-do' list, I am always making 'To-do' list.

Chambers:

What advice and encouragement would you give to a young entrepreneur?

Stephens:

Continual education. Just find everything and read everything you can about money, success, in addition to all the nuts and bolts about owning a business like book keeping, accounting, retirement, you know, all the nuts and bolts of owning a business, just a continual education on self improvement, learning to know yourself better, learning what your weaknesses are, so that you can find a person who will complement or do the things that you don't like or can't do, and allow yourself to do the things that you can do and the things that you like to do. When you are doing the things that you like to do and do well, it makes you more at peace and you are not so frustrated trying to do things that you just don't like to do or don't know how to do.

Chambers:

What does it take to be a great leader?

Stephens:

Example, you live by example, courage, setting goals, taking and breaking large goals down into small goals and achieving each one at a time, continually showing appreciation to those that are helping you that you are leading. One of the best examples that I ever read was of General Patton, because he was a general but he always went down into his troops and talked to each one of them individually and that is the sign of a great leader, someone that can talk to and listen to other people and take their suggestions to heart, and sometimes they are right.

Chambers:
What inspires you to do what you do?

Stephens:

Being able to help other people enjoy life more, feel less stressed and aggravated, allowing people to enjoy their families and pursue their dreams and not just go to work, come home, eat, go to sleep and go to work and spend hours on traffic. I enjoy teaching, I enjoy seeing other people, the light on their face when they get it and they see that their life is going to change.

Chambers:
What is the greatest risk you have ever taken and was it worth it?

Stephens:

Well, I guess that would be when I decided to go for my pilot's license. One of the very first classes that I enrolled in was The Ground School where you learn all the basics and all the rules and regulations of flying and the very first week, the instructor said, "In order to learn, you got to get into an airplane, you got to actually fly." So I went to enroll but I was still afraid, you know, it was way beyond me, flying an airplane is complicated. So I would walk into a flight school and asked the person behind the counter, they didn't acknowledge me, but then a half a minute or so, I would turn and walk back out. And I did that about 6 times, until the last one, I was at the airport closest to where I live, in Long Beach at the Long Beach airport, and the guy behind the counter, acknowledged me and said, "Can I help you?" almost immediately and so when he said that, I didn't have a chance to turn around and walk out and so I enrolled in it and, oh, yeah, it is definitely worth it. I love flying. That is something I wanted to do since I was about 14. My dad was a pilot, he loved aviation, so I guess I kind of inherited it from him. Whenever I feel stupid or feel like I am incompetent or whatever, I just remember I can fly, I am not stupid.

Chambers:
If you could do anything and you knew you would not fail, what would you do?

Stephens:
Well, I would like to get into the astronaut program. I would like to be an astronaut.

Chambers:
If you can share any advice with someone, what would it be?

Stephens:
Don't be down on yourself, don't listen to the little voice in the back

of your head that keeps telling you, you are not good enough, you are not worthwhile, you know, people don't like you, you are too ugly, all of those negative things, just try and not listen to them. Find any way you can to get rid of them.

Chambers:

What kind of legacy do you want to leave?

Stephens:

That I benefited humanity, that some how humanity was elevated because of the work I did, either happier or more successful, less stressed, more joyful, some how elevated.

Chambers:

In all honesty, your story as lifted me and will continue to lift those who learn about you.

Grace Stephens
79 E. Daily Drive, #241
Camarillo, CA 93010

Chapter 6

Jeff Roldan
Film Producer & Cinematographer

David E. Chambers (Chambers):
Jeff, how did you get into the film industry?

Jeff Roldan (Roldan)
I've always been into filmmaking, even since I was little. I think everyone has a thing that they know they're good at, or something that they dream about when they're a kid. When I was little I would envision myself being a filmmaker. Even though I wasn't really in the industry, mentally I was into creating motion pictures, and envisioned making motion pictures to entertain people. I'd say officially, you get

into the film industry when you make your first film; but mentally, I think I've always been there... right from when I was young.

Chambers:

That's interesting! Most people have passions and desires as a child, but they don't take it all the way through; what drove you to take that desire as a child and make your first movie?

Roldan:

I've never thought about doing anything else other than what I was passionate about. With parents who supported me and loved my entertaining antics, they helped fuel my desire to keep on this path. In fact, I didn't want to go to college unless it was for filmmaking.

I think the thing that drove me to become a filmmaker was always having that vision, and also following what you're passionate about. There are other things that I like to do, hobbies etc., but the one thing I truly love and can consistently turn to is creating movies. So, I think it's just a matter of following what actually drives you in your life. With endless opportunities to create visual stories, I've never had a desire to pursue anything else. So, I guess it's just come naturally.

Chambers:

When you have that passion and that drive, there are still days that are difficult – you need to push through when you're going through school, or let's say you're on set and you're having a tough time – what do you do for yourself personally, to help you stay focused on your goals and your dreams?

Roldan:

I turn to other people's creative works for inspiration. I love movies and music and often, just watching or hearing an amazing new sound, will lead me to think how I can incorporate or expand on a great new idea. When I see a never before told story, it becomes a catalyst to all of the ideas swirling around in my head. In that respect, I don't think anything is truly original because mankind has always used the inspiration of those before them to create the next great work of art or story.

Chambers:

When you're on set and you've got to organize people, and you've got to get the right shot and the right lighting, it takes a lot of leadership skills to accomplish that. What do you define as a great leader?

Roldan:

I think a great leader is somebody who can earn the respect and confidence of others so that they will follow, not totally blindly, but based on their experience. A leader should constantly radiate confidence and can be trusted by other people in situations when they look to you for a decision to be made. The more that others see that your decisions lead to a successful outcome, the more willing they will be to follow your lead.

Kindness goes a long way as well. So often people in the movie industry forget that politeness is still an essential leadership trait. I find that the best people will want to continue working with you on the next project, if you treated them well on the previous project.

Chambers:

As a leader, when times get tough, how do you stay focused? What do you do to motivate your troops?

Roldan:

I stay focused by being organized. I try to keep a business journal of important tasks and idea's with me at all times. I break the project down into days and weeks. That helps me maintain a hold on the bigger picture.

True motivation (a better phrase would be inspiration to action) comes from taking a step back and focusing on what's truly trying to be accomplished. Once everyone can see what the potential outcome will be, and what the best steps are to accomplish that goal, it is then easier to move forward in unity. I try to do this by sharing with everyone. If the person in charge of lighting is inspired by the project he or she is working on, then it makes it that much more exciting and energizing to be on that project. The trick, however, is to get everyone to see that vision of the goal, or at least get them to see it the way I do. This is what truly motivates people. To do this I show sample movies of what others have done, share music, show drawings, anything to convey what I see in my head so they can see it too. Once they can see it, energy for the project comes naturally.

Chambers:

How do you define success?

Roldan:

I would say that success is self-defined. If you want something in life, or you're passionate about something, success is actually being able to carry out that passion or that desire and letting nothing get in your way.

I think true success is when you accomplish the things that you set out to do, despite what others have said or thought, and as long as you feel passionate about it, I think that that's success. Basically, if you view yourself as successful, you are! It doesn't matter how the world defines it. It's your own success, who cares what they think.

Chambers:

You've enjoyed some success in the film industry – what originally inspired you to get into films?

Roldan:

Well, my Mom said that when I was one year old, I was inspired by Star Wars at the drive-in movies, when we first watched it... but I can't say that that was necessarily the experience that inspired me to get into filmmaking.

Originally, I wanted to be an actor. I did a lot of acting when I was really young but I realized that you don't have as much control over the story and basically you're playing a part that someone else has defined. I think filmmaking came more naturally to me because I know what it takes to entertain others. I love to see people laugh based on something I've created and more recently, I've enjoyed seeing people cry with inspirational stories I've been able to depict. So initially, it started with that desire to entertain; but more and more, it's become something where I just want to touch people's lives.

Chambers:

What is a film that inspired you to create movies?

Roldan:

Steven Spielberg's Jurassic Park was the movie that opened my eyes to filmmaking – I watched that movie a dozen times in the local dollar theater when I was in high school. What I loved about it and what was so inspiring about that movie to me – aside from the visual effects – was that it took you into a completely different world and you left the theater feeling as though you had gone on that adventure yourself. It was energizing. And I think to me, a good movie is one that can offer you a different perspective on your life through viewing the lives of other, even if it is fictional.

Chambers:

Where did you get your education for films?

Roldan:

My education for films began in Junior High, when my dad brought home a camcorder he borrowed from work. I remember staying up all night figuring out how to get music synced with video (because at that time, there were no computer editing systems, and I was a Junior High student without any equipment) To me, that was huge – something as simple as putting music with video change the feeling of what you were viewing. Through that, and other self teaching moments, my education in making movies began. My formal education would come a little later, when I went to San Diego State University and got a BA there in Television, Film and New Media. But my education, for me, began long before that.

In fact, I was in high school when I started my first production company. In my senior year, we produced a series of videos for the high school. I had a group of about 4-5 cameramen, and we did sports highlights videos. Along with that we produced a Senior Video – which was a documentary/narrative. For a high school business, it was very successful and a great opportunity to learn.

Chambers:

What has been your greatest A-Ha moment in business?

Roldan:

One A-Ha moment that I can remember distinctly, came very recently, in the making of the film I-ology. I realized that you can take any idea and turn it into a movie to teach an audience. Now, whether or not it's going to be a good film is another question. But open the encyclopedia and put your finger down on a topic – there is a story behind that topic. What you do with that idea, the angle you take, obviously makes it a good or bad, marketable or unmarketable, inspiring or just flat out boring. You don't necessarily need a crew of hundreds and hundreds of people.

Look at Morgan Spurlock and what he did with 'Super Size Me'. Essentially, it was a guy with a camcorder and an idea. I know that I was born in this era because of the fact that technology would be so accessible. You can start today if you want by writing down ideas. Everyone has at one time or another said 'that would make a good movie.' Well, there's your idea! And so, my 'A-Ha' moment came during the film I-ology when I discovered that it's just the matter of taking an idea and putting it down on paper or brainstorming, and then start building it. That's exactly the process that was involved with the film I-ology. The concept was brought before me and we developed it, we started filming and started telling stories. This can be done quite simply if you have just a few tools at your disposal.

Chambers:

When you start a film, do you have to know the end before the beginning? I would assume that when you do a film, you don't always have every answer – you don't always know when you're going to get the best shot and the best lighting. Do you have to know that to begin?

Roldan:

No, I don't think you need to know the end and all the in's and out's. I think you just have to have an idea and be open to the fact that it might change. There are even a lot of feature films that have changed the ending down to the last few weeks of production. I think you don't have to know the in's and out's; I just think you need to know what you want people to get out of it, and in case of a documentary, if you have a message you want them to learn, if you want them to feel a certain way, or if you're trying to sway them in a certain direction, then you should be open to change if that can be better accomplished.

Chambers:

What advice or encouragement would you give to someone who's just starting in business, or in the film industry?

Roldan:

The advice that I would give to somebody aspiring to do film production and get into the filmmaking industry would be to make good contacts – network like crazy. Don't be a jerk; be a friendly person and that will open up doors for you, because people remember your kindness. Help people get what they want. You don't need to be a "people pleaser", but you need to be able to be agreeable. Even when you want things your own way, perhaps try to see things another way. I think networking and getting to work with other people is important. They always say that it's who you know, and not what you know…this is very true especially in the filmmaking industry. Networking is going to be the biggest thing you can ever do.

Another bit of advice I would give to a filmmaker would be to just do it – just start today, and start simple. If you're passionate about filmmaking and your idea then you won't find it hard to dedicate yourself to your project. If you don't have your idea yet, get lots of practice with other people's projects. Even if you have friends who need something shot, take those productions and try to make them big… try to make them bigger than they are, and you'll find yourself stretching yourself.

Chambers:

What's the greatest reward in doing what you do?

Roldan:

The greatest reward in doing what I do is watching the end product. When you sit down and hit 'Play' and you just love what you've done, it is so rewarding. Also, when you get to see others watch it and they enjoy it, then that's equally rewarding. To see people laughing when they're supposed to laugh, and crying when they're supposed to cry means you've got it right and touched them in someway.

Chambers:

What is the greatest risk you've ever taken, and was it worth it?

Roldan:

When I was just out of college everybody in the television-film program wanted to be directors or involved in these huge productions.

Actually, I wasn't too interested in that at the time. I was focusing more on trying to make a living. So I started a business despite everyone telling me I had to move to Hollywood to get a job. Business was slow at first but I made it a personal goal one year to gross $50,000, which for me at the time was a lot of revenue, especially when my gross revenue averaged around $15,000. So, I took a risk. I could have gone and gotten work and commuted and spent hours and hours in the car, and had late nights and less time with my family; but I was able to capitalize on the business that was around me, in the San Diego area, versus commuting up to Los Angeles. And I found that beneficial. That risk has carried me into my own production company versus riding on the coattails of someone else.

Chambers:

Having taken that risk in building your own production company, what areas do you focus on at this point?

Roldan:

Currently my focus is on utilizing the skills that I've been acquiring over the past few years. I am specializing in me/myself as a filmmaker, as a consultant. My ability to bring out the emotion in projects is opening the door to a variety of projects. People can bring me into their ideas for production and with my skills and my talent make it a reality.

Chambers:

What are your goals?

Roldan:

My goals and future plans are to continue to make inspirational productions, to build up a client base of people who consistently come to me for consulting or to produce their own films, and also to independently be able to produce things that I want and self-fund those productions.

I also want to grow my other two production businesses and make them able to run themselves.

Chambers:

If you could share any advice with someone, what would it be?

Roldan:

The advice I would share with somebody is to not give up on an idea, no matter what other people think about it. If you can see it in your head, don't give up on it. That vision is yours and the most valuable thing that you can carry with you into a production.

Chambers:

What type of legacy do you want to leave?

Roldan:

I'd like to leave a legacy of inspirational work – things that influence people for the good, productions that help people get through hard times, or productions that inform people and change people's life because of the information that was conveyed. I find a lot of satisfaction in that. If my work can continue to influence others long after I am gone then that would be a great accomplishment.

For more information, visit:

www.jeffroldan.com

Chapter 7

Marvin Montillano
Real Estate Investor/Coach

David E. Chambers (Chambers):
You are a successful real estate investor. What brought you to make the
transition from working a W-2 job as a physical therapist to becoming
a successful entrepreneur?

Marvin Montillano (Montillano):
It turns out that I'm someone who is never satisfied. I've always tried
to achieve more. As I was working my W-2 position, I realized there
was a ceiling to what I was doing. After I'd been in that career for a
little while, I was asking myself, "What is the next step?" One of my

instructors in physical therapy school actually gave me a ceiling. She said, "Because of the 'manual' labor involved in hands-on physical therapy, only plan on being a clinician for 7 to 10 years." My next logical step, to minimize the 'hands-on' work and potential physical stress, would be to become a physical therapy manager, administrator, or educator.

When I thought about that, it just didn't excite me because I couldn't see any real growth that I could achieve for myself in those roles. Ultimately, when I saw other therapists who were 10, 20, 30 years into the profession, they weren't anywhere that I wanted to be. That was a reality check, right there. Growing up in a family accustomed to working government jobs (i.e., military, county jobs, etc.), I was really looking to generate an income and a lifestyle that was far beyond what I was used to. I guess I went a step further by going into the healthcare industry which requires more education and pays more, but I found out early in my career that there was a ceiling there, too, and it turned out that my lifestyle wasn't too much different than that of my parents.

So, when I was introduced to real estate investing by a friend and others who came into my life through my physical therapy work, I knew I had to learn something different. I saw the lifestyle and financial freedom they had, and I thought, "Okay, I want to be able to achieve that." I decided that by utilizing real estate as an investment vehicle, I could create that type of success and lifestyle for myself. I jumped in and started exploring real estate investing through whatever books and seminars I could access.

Chambers:

Was it difficult for your family to accept you going in a different direc-

tion and rising above their current level, and did they discourage you from going into investing?

Montillano:

Not a huge opposition to it, but rather, questions and skepticism—particularly from my mother who always worries. When I started getting into real estate investing, and not really spending much time working as a physical therapist, she thought it was odd. She would ask me if I was doing okay financially. That was the most important thing; she wanted to know that I was financially secure. To her, that was more important than being happy at my job.

I was able to show my 'real estate investing vision' to a few family members, but ultimately, no one had the belief or confidence in it that I had. That reaction from them was somewhat of a downer. I could see the possibilities and knew they could see the possibilities, too. But, they just couldn't see themselves moving forward with me or my vision, whether it was because of fear, an inability to step out of their comfort zones, or a lack of understanding. I had to accept that not everyone is cut out to be an entrepreneur.

Chambers:

When you decided to take the leap of faith and really go into investing, what was the biggest challenge you came up against?

Montillano:

Personally, the biggest challenge for me was learning all the new information and becoming familiar with it. I knew nothing of investing. I just knew basic principles about why I should invest from books, but not how. Once I finally applied my new education, and established a local network of real estate mentors and real estate professionals to support me, my confidence level in investing was very high. It was also a challenge that I was still working in a full-time W-2 job when I first started while building the investment side of my business. I had to figure out how to *make* the time to learn to be an investor and then start networking with the right individuals. It took perseverance and persistence for me to work myself out of employment especially with my mindset at that time. I had to totally change my way of thinking.

Chambers:

You've mentioned the power of a mentor; when someone is looking for a mentor, what should they look for?

Montillano:

First of all, you want to look for someone who is already doing what you want to be doing, someone who has already gone through the process, and who can help you avoid the pitfalls. You need someone to help you with your mindset. I think the key is finding a mentor who can understand where you are and where you want to be. If a mentor can identify with you on that level, it's really going to help you.

A great mentor will be able to prepare you for challenges and say, "Hey, you're going to experience this…You have this obstacle coming over the horizon, but just keep pressing forward…Don't get caught up in fear." This is important because a lot of people don't know how many challenges will come up in their path. Your mentor can provide the reassurance to you that, *"This is the process. You're going to have opposition from all different angles, but do not quit."* He or she can help encourage you to break through, and reach your goal.

So, having a mentor, or even multiple mentors for different aspects of your life (physical, mental, relational, financial, and spiritual) allows you to become empowered and a better human being.

Chambers:

As a successful investor, I know you've mentored many people. What does it take to be a good mentor?

Montillano:

To be a good mentor you have to have leadership ability. It's not that you are someone who has always been the leader of every team or organization that you've been a part of, but that you are willing to take risks that others are not willing to take. You don't just talk the talk. You envision greater reward from opportunity that involves risk versus the adversity you face.

A leadership role is something I've been able to grow into. When I first started out, I was very much a follower—following my mentor. I was doing the things that he did, and going through some struggles, particularly in terms of my mindset. In going through that process, I started to understand who I had to be and what I needed to do in order to become a leader. Now I'm in that role, mentoring and coaching others, and I understand now that in order for me to accomplish something I've never done, I had to become somebody I never knew I could be. Once I saw that in myself, then I was able to transfer that belief to other individuals, letting them know that I started out just like them. But through education, mentorship, and coaching, I was able to grow to who I am today.

So for me mentoring is showing people who they can become versus who they currently are. I help them overcome the definitions and limitations they have of themselves based on what profession or upbringing they've had in the past. For example, someone might say to me, "I'm *just* a manager." I want to help that person see the possibility of who they can become—an investor, or whoever it is that they choose to be. I guide them to seek the things that would create opportunity, as I did when I sought to create the successful investor within me. Through that process, I became a better person and I continue to develop myself.

I love the personal growth that is happening now, and I know that my growth will never stop. I let go of the idea that I would eventually reach a certain level in my life and say, "That's it. I've arrived." I know now that I must keep learning, growing, and improving—it's an unending process.

One thing I bring to mentoring is getting people to reflect on the question, "What is my purpose?" I remember sitting in traffic on my way to my W-2 job, asking myself, "Why am I driving 45 minutes in this traffic? There's got to be more to what I do in this life than this. I'm not reaching out to anybody just working for my family and myself. I'm not creating greater things that could bless others. I'm not touching other people's lives in a way that matters to me."

In my profession I was helping people, but I felt so limited. I couldn't see myself helping anyone outside of my scope of physical therapy practice. I was stuck in a system—'X 'amount of visits, 'X 'amount of reimbursement—that I didn't have control over. I wanted to do something where I could really serve and impact people's lives on another level.

Chambers:

What's the secret combination to finding success in investing in real estate?

....

Montillano:

Learning the strategy you want to implement and mastering it. Mentoring with somebody, and even partnering with someone who has been using the strategy successfully with a way to duplicate the system. If you don't have a system, it will be a process of trial and error, and you'll never have any focus or success. If you can focus on a system that has worked for others, you'll increase your profitability. Don't stray from the system. If it works, don't try to reinvent the wheel.

The other thing that is important is knowing who you are as a person, because certain strategies may be suited for one personality type, but not another. It's good to explore a lot of different strategies and find one that's right for you. If you are thinking about short sales, shadow a successful investor to gain an understanding of short sales and how this type of transaction works, then you'll know whether or not you have what it takes to be successful. Maybe you are the kind of person who'd be better off buying properties at auction, fix and flip, or wholesaling. In any case, find something you love. Success always comes down to activity that is pleasurable, not painful, because it will show in the income that you generate.

Chambers:

We all know there are ups and downs in real estate investing. What techniques do you use to pull yourself through the "down" periods?

Montillano:

I listen to and read a lot of personal development material, and seek out people who are continually experiencing success and overcoming challenges. Personal development is something I do on a daily basis. It is a type of "mindset maintenance" activity for me. It helps me maintain my focus on moving forward, because a lot of the obstacles that you come across in investing and entrepreneurship are things that can hang you up, personally and financially. If you wallow in it, it will take you out of your game. So, when I can plug myself into information on success, then I understand that what I am experiencing is part of the process and is temporary, and that the only way I will break myself out of the slump is by moving forward and being productive.

Another thing I do to stay in 'success mode' is planning out my day where it is predictable. I plan out my entire day—how many hours I will be spending in each activity, whether it is personal time, family time or business time. After I've gone through that day, I have a great sense of accomplishment and have quantifiable results for my productivity.

For example, I do a lot of prospecting calls, and I have an accountability report that I utilize. I'm able to see my productivity, whether it is 50 calls or 100 calls in a day to book appointments with potential real estate prospects. I see my results and I know what it takes, in terms of the number of calls I must make, to get a certain number of appointments booked. The more appointments I book the greater my income potential.

Through this process, I know what it takes to create specific results on a regular basis. It's predictable, measurable, and therefore I can move forward even if I get 30 people who are not interested in setting an appointment. I know if I keep going, I'll get a booked appointment. This is something I really had to learn to be disciplined and implement before I started seeing results. Otherwise, I let the fear of rejection hold me back. I have overcome that so making 50 or

100 calls a week doesn't faze me anymore.

Chambers:

When people get stuck in fear, what can they do to overcome it?

Montillano:

When someone gets stuck in fear, they need to ask themselves, "Why am I afraid?" Then they must ask themselves what the risks of the activity are and start weighing the pros and cons. What will they achieve by doing it? What will they achieve (or lose) if they don't do it? If they can list the answers and see the potential benefits of 'doing' versus the consequences of 'not doing', it helps to break through the fear.

When I've done this, I've always ended up with the certainty that there are greater, more satisfying benefits in doing the activity, versus not doing it. If we don't do anything, we've already created the result that is no more than the status quo. We can start creating scenarios in our minds, and then start getting down on ourselves, which leads to greater fear and inactivity.

I've always seen the other side as, "If I do participate in this, this is what can happen; these are the types of people I can meet; these are the types of deals that I can come across." I've seen that happen. I've had the experience of not contacting certain people because of fear that they won't be interested in my investment. But when I finally picked up the phone, and said, "This is the deal I have. Are you interested in it?" They've said "Yes, that's great. I'd be more than willing to do that."

Sometimes I've been afraid to ask, "How much do you want to invest in this deal?" thinking that they may only want to put in a couple thousand dollars. One investor answered the question by saying, "On the first deal with you...$250,000 to $500,000." I didn't expect that and if I hadn't asked, I would have never known. Now I am bird-dogging for deals that fit that profile. I'm not fearful of contacting people anymore because I know that it is the key to growing my business.

Chambers:

What has been your greatest "Ah-ha" moment in your business?

Montillano:

My greatest "Ah-ha" moment came from one of my mentors. In fact, had this mentor not come into my investment group, I might not have had the success and risen to the level that I have in the last few years.

One thing that I had always done in my life was transfer blame to other people. If I wasn't having success, it was because someone else wasn't connecting me to the right person, or presenting me with the right opportunity, or something along those lines. It was in my mind that 'other people' weren't supporting me in the way that they should.

What I found out was that if I wasn't having success, it was because *I wasn't working*—I wasn't connecting, I wasn't networking, I wasn't utilizing my own resources. It really took my mentor's lesson for me to realize that "if it was going to be, it was up to me." He taught me that to get through any new venture, it's always going to take a four-stage process.

If I hadn't learned this process, I wouldn't have known that I was ultimately accountable for my results.

That's the most important thing that I've learned about being in business. If you're going to make it happen, only YOU are going to make it happen—no one else.

Chambers:

What advice would you give to someone who wants to get into real estate investing?

Montillano:

I would definitely recommend getting the right education—the kind where you are able to immediately apply what you learn. No matter what the cost, if the value is there, it's worth it. You need the knowledge, and you need coaching along with the education. It's crucial to have someone oversee what you're doing as you move through the strategy being implemented. Of course, you have to do the work, but at least you'll have the right people in your professional network to contact for guidance. That's vital. Your business will be more profitable as a result of being coached *around* the pitfalls. Essentially, someone who wants to succeed in real estate needs to have a system and a team in place to support them.

Networking with real estate professionals, real estate brokers, title companies, bank officers, mortgage brokers and especially those who invest in real estate themselves is helpful. They understand the transactions and can teach you about the system. You may find a lot of deals, but if you don't have a network to plug into that knows what you're doing, then you're dead in the water and in danger of losing your deal and your money. To avoid this, have your team in place.

Chambers:

What inspires you?

Montillano:

People who achieve things that they never knew were possible—people who have a 'vision' for greatness and go after it inspire me. There is a lot of untapped wealth within a person, and when I see someone release his or her potential and achieve something amazing, it's very inspiring. It's great to see how they have grown because they made a decision to achieve their dream despite their circumstances. When I hear their stories of great adversity and how they remained persistent and kept a spirit of faith throughout their journey, it truly inspires me.

Chambers:

What type of legacy do you want to leave?

Montillano:

The legacy I want to leave is one of true financial independence—I want my family to have true wealth in all areas of life. I hope that they will learn from my experiences and my coaching so that they have the knowledge and the inspiration to keep building, growing, and creating.

My family's journey began with my father's decision to join the US military and come to the US from a third world country. It is because of that decision that I am here with virtually unlimited opportunities. I have the choices and opportunities to be, do, and have more than most people in the world today. Sometimes I feel like my family takes that for granted. But if I can change the family mindset from one of mere survival to one of abundance, I can change the way we move through our lives, from a life of mere existence to a life of joyful creation, contribution, and service.

I also want to leave a legacy of charitable giving to those less fortunate. Having my entire family be a part of that would be wonderful. I want us all to know what it really feels like to give from the abundance of our hearts and our finances. If we can all stamp our names on the contributions we've made for others, whether it is through service or through finances, then that would solidify for me my vision of a noble legacy for my family.

Marvin Montillano
24910 Las Brisas Road, Suite 118
Murrieta, CA 92562
951-704-2215

marvin@newwealthadvisors.com
www.newwealthadvisors.com

Chapter 8

Stacy Kirch
Success Coach + College Counselor

David E. Chambers (Chambers)
What inspired you to become a success coach?

Stacy Kirch (Kirch):
It fills me up when I can help someone move towards becoming the person they are truly meant to be, and pursue their passions and dreams. Looking back, I can remember teachers and coaches who completely squashed my spirit. I actually felt worse about myself and less motivated to do my best work as a result of seeing them. On the other hand, I had teachers and counselors who were inspirational and

helped me to become my best self. They came from a place of abundance where one's soul, spirit, and love spills over to others. I strive to emulate those teachers and counselors by coming from a place of abundance and inspiring others as well. I want to be someone who has a long lasting positive, even life changing effect on people.

Chambers:

While becoming a success coach for college athletes and other successful people in your community how did you break through fear or overcome others saying you couldn't achieve? Was there a turning point when you decided I'm going to achieve no matter what?

Kirch:

There wasn't any one particular turning point; it was more a sequence of turning points that built up to where I decided I could not continue to squash my own spirit. Instead of being happy, I was miserable. And I made a decision: If I wanted to be successful and happy, something had to change. I started asking questions. Since what I was doing at the time was not working, I began to ask things like, "What can I do differently? How can I get past my insecurities? How can I get past what other people say and stop letting it paralyze me?" The more I asked myself these questions, the more I found out about myself. I was then able to ask myself questions like, "When have I felt successful?" and "When do I feel most alive and passionate?" At that point, I began to move towards things where I had a history of success and used them as my springboard. I started seeking out the right people–mentors who could help me pursue what I wanted, as opposed to hindering it. I was very careful about who I sought for help and support because I had experienced reaching out to the wrong people and getting my spirit crushed. I quickly learned that includes being cautious regarding family and friends when seeking help, support, advice, or counsel. I started to establish a new support system, including a counselor, who helped tremendously in terms of allowing me to be okay with my feelings and accepting them. I was able to release my feelings instead of denying them. For me this was a significant step.

Chambers:

When someone is looking for a mentor or success coach, what attributes should they look for? How should they interview the person to make sure they are getting the right information? What recommendations would you give to finding the right mentors?

Kirch:

First, when looking for a success coach or mentor, be very clear about what you want. Even though it's one of the most important life skills, it's very difficult for most of us to ask for help. Knowing what you want help with makes it that much easier. So I would definitely start by getting clarity on your wants. Secondly, and this may sound obvious, but I would definitely start with determining who is *willing* to be a mentor. Keep in mind that simply because someone is very knowledgeable about her area of expertise does not mean she is a good fit for mentoring. You are asking for and taking the time and energy of your mentor. When you find a mentor who is a willing and energetic participant, you have already done much to set the stage for your success. Thirdly, seek out someone who is passionate and has demonstrated success in the area that you want to pursue. The wonderful thing about mentors is they have been where you are trying to go.

They have already proven themselves to be successful and are now able to teach you based on their experiences.

You want to find someone who has the ability to not only encourage, but challenge you; someone who not only guides and teaches, but more importantly, gives you opportunities to achieve success yourself by allowing you to do things on your own without them doing it for you. My best mentors are masters of balancing challenge and support. Sometimes they have been critics helping me to move forward, and other times they have been my biggest cheerleader, reminding me of what I am capable of doing. When those I work with hit "lows" and start to waiver in their beliefs of their dreams, I both push them and pick them up. There is an art to finding when the challenge or the support is more important.

Chambers:

Why do you think people get so scared to actually ask for help or to find a mentor?

Kirch:

When people come from a deficit place and being fearful, instead of coming from a place of passion, love and want, they are afraid to ask for help. Most people – in every area of their lives–come from an obligation status. People often say "I should", "I have to", "I need to"– all of these statements are fear-based and not want-based. Someone who is coming from a deficit place where they may feel trapped or overwhelmed or "less than" or "not good enough," do not feel worthy of receiving help, much less asking for it.

What I've learned in my life and seeing from others who are successful is that the best way to break through the fear of asking for help is to simply ask someone – anyone –for help. Just like with anything, the more you practice, the easier it gets. When I started asking for help and *expecting I would get it*, an amazing thing happened: I got it. My requests for help were not met with judgment or "I can't believe you're asking" statements or even "no's." My requests were met, time after time, with a resounding "Yes!" I quickly learned there are a lot more people who want to help compared to those who do not. And if you get a "no", it's okay. It's better to find out quickly where you will and won't get help. That "no" is just another step towards the person who will say "yes". This helps to get over the "no" quickly. However when you're coming from that deficit and fear place, it's difficult to do that–which is why mentors, counselors, and success coaches are so important.

Chambers:

What kinds of questions should people ask themselves to start thinking differently about their life?

Kirch:

Some good questions to ask to begin to start thinking differently about your life are: "In a perfect world, what would you want? If you knew you couldn't fail, what would you do? What is possible? When are you happiest? When do you feel most passionate? When do you feel most *you*? When do you feel like you are exactly who you are meant to be and you are in love with yourself? What are you doing? What does it look like; paint yourself a picture." These are just a few of the questions I would ask to begin thinking differently about life. And our lives are directly proportional to the quality of the questions we ask, so start asking questions that will bring you what you want.

Chambers:

How can we focus on the abundance of life?

Kirch:

There is no simple answer to that question. In my journey what helped me to focus on the abundance of life was first recognizing my feelings and allowing them to come. I believe that until you are able to acknowledge your feelings and feel them you will not be able to move forward. When people say, "just be happy" or "just be positive" or "just focus on the positive," it's not that easy. Many times people are aching for someone to validate their feelings–telling them they have every right to feel the way they do and it's okay. If I'm mad, I have every right to be mad, if I'm sad, I have every right to be sad, or if I'm a hurt, I have every right to be hurt. After acknowledging and feeling, then I can ask myself how this emotion is serving me. What do I want to do about it? And I can flip it on its head and start coming from a state of *want* instead of fear. I focus on what I want instead of what I want to avoid. I ask myself "What do I want?" instead of constantly spending time and energy looking at what I *don't* want. Abundance comes from how we *feel*. If I can feel it and validate it I can move forward. It's not about my thoughts; it's about my feelings. It's about moving from the deficit place to where I want to be.

Chambers:

When you are feeling down, what techniques do you recommend in order to switch to an abundance mentality?

Kirch:

First, have at your fingertips reminders of past successes, accomplishments, and proud moments in which you were amazed by your own achievements and who you are when you are your best self. Remembering those past successes helps to encourage future successes. It's a way of reminding yourself that you can have future successes as well. The past successes are your spring board. I absolutely believe in the truth of "success breeds more success".

A second thing I recommend is utilizing the power of music. Music is a huge energy shifter and energy booster. It's something that can easily lift you up instead of dragging you down. Be mindful that this does not mean to rush out of your emotions if you are not ready. Use music when you are ready to let go of feelings like being angry and hurt and sad. Don't' rush this work. Otherwise, you'll say things like, "I'm fine" when your emotions are still eating you up. When you are ready to let go (which happens after validating your emotions), when you are ready to get out of being stuck or fixating on anger or pain and you want to do something else that will bring you joy and feelings of being happy, music can be a great tool to move you forward.

Another technique is using books as a source of inspiration. I'm a huge fan of quotations of the day. I subscribe to a service that provides an emailed quotation or story every day. It's amazing how those quotations and stories and affirmations match up with a particular need at just the right time with what's going on in my life.

Spending time with people who love me unconditionally is another awesome strategy. I don't have to do or say anything when I'm in the midst of those who love me simply because I breathe. I know they are going to love me for exactly who I am. They are willing to listen and allow me a safe place to land so I can feel anything that I'm feeling without judgment. I don't have to rush my emotions and I don't have to feel okay or good so that I'm meeting their comfort level. It's important to have people who allow you to be down when you need to be. Having the space to be down allows me and provides the opportunities for me to then move forward.

Chambers:

How do you focus and get clarity in what you really want?

Kirch:

To focus and get clarity on what I really want I ask myself questions. I use a process of writing my wants down on paper. At the top, I'll write "What do I Want" and have several categories underneath. For example, categories might include personal, career, family, recreational, physical, financial, and spiritual. I also include a time context. For example, instead of just "What do I Want" I may write "What do I Want Today?" Your time context could be daily, monthly, and yearly – whatever timeframe you'd like it to be. Then, I'll brainstorm and jot down all my wants. Using the 80/20 principle which states 20% of what you actually do is going to reap 80 % of the benefits. Using this principle, I narrow my list by what has the highest priority. Focusing only on the top 20% allows me to focus on just a few things instead of trying to do it all. If I come from a perfectionist mentality of trying to do everything perfectly, I end up doing nothing well. The 80/20 principle is helpful in that I'm able to focus on a few things that I want to do and I'm then able to do them really well. Frequently, I go back and review the list asking myself "Is this really something I want?" And inevitably, the things that I most want rise to the top again and again.

I want to help motivate people and help them pursue their passions in life. I want to live my life in such a way that I become a vehicle for people to become passionate, encompass love and have overflowing abundance. I want my life to be a demonstration to others. When I'm so passionate and so full of love and overflowing with abundance, I'm not only able to tell people, I'm able to show them.

Most importantly as a parent it's important that I show my children lessons I want them to learn. Telling them is not enough. How can I tell them "You can be and do anything you in life" if I'm not doing it myself?

Chambers:

How do the techniques you've mastered as a success coach apply to raising a family?

Kirch:

All of the same things that apply to any success apply to raising a family, which is first and foremost to stop and listen. In order to be in the moment, you must stop whatever else it is that you are doing. And then listen to what is being said. I want to really be in the moment and present with whomever I'm with. So with my kids I really work on being in the moment with them. I'm not trying to multi-task, doing a hundred things at the same time. I don't do that well. And I don't think most people do that well. I think when you are focused on a deeper level, you tend to have more success than you would by spreading yourself too thin.

As a Mom, I really work to come from abundance rather than deficit, so I work to meet *my* needs and be happy myself–*first*. Initially, this may sound selfish. Actually, it's one of the best things I can do for my family. When I'm happy, I'm then in a better position to help my kids and husband be happy. I'm coming from abundance and so I'm able to give abundance. Otherwise if I were coming deficit, I may do things I don't intend such as yelling, being cranky, or having little patience. My husband and I both try to pursue what we want in life, not at the expense of our children, but because of our children. We want to demonstrate and give those same opportunities to them.

Chambers:

What does it take to be a true leader in this society?

Kirch:

A true leader has the ability to listen. A true leader is confident in who they are and are able to be their best self and can help support others to be their best selves. Surrounding themselves with those who specifically can help them grow are characteristics of a true leader, realizing they aren't perfect at everything and that the more you surround yourself with other amazing people, the more knowledge you gain. True leaders understand there is something to learn from everyone.

For example, my husband is a college baseball coach and when he surrounds himself with an amazing assistant coaching staff, this helps him to be that much better of a leader. When he allows them to do what they do best without trying to control everything or micromanaging them, their gifts and talents shine through. When he trusts them to do their best work and communicates his belief that they are capable, everyone starts operating on a best self level – this elevates the level of success for the entire team and makes everyone better.

A true leader has the ability to bring out passion in others by moving people towards their wants instead hindering it by placing "shoulds" on them. I think when administrators or managers try to micromanage everything and say, "You have to do this," whether you want to or not, it is not very productive and it's not going to lead to any long-term success. I think true leaders are the ones who can bring people to a place of wanting to do things and capitalize on their passions. And lastly I think leaders don't take themselves too seriously. They have the ability to laugh at themselves, while at the same time treating what others say and feel with the utmost respect and consideration.

Chambers:
How do you define success?

Kirch:
I define success as having the ability to be happy in any circumstance. True happiness is based on how you feel internally and not the external circumstances surrounding you. Being perfectly me is what makes me happy because I'm coming from a state of abundance. I strive to come from this state 100% of the time. I fail to do this just about daily... *AND* it's what I strive to do.

Chambers:
When times are tough and you find it difficult to focus what steps do you take to bring yourself back in line and focused?

Kirch:
I have mantras and questions that I ask myself over and over again. I had them written on a 3x5 card and would carry them in my pocket. After a few years of this, I eventually had the mantras and questions so engrained that I no longer needed the card. Now it's automatic, so when I recognize that I'm getting off focus I ask myself, how am I feeling right now? I'll go through the six main emotions, which are

being happy, sad, mad, hurt, scared, and ashamed. (Ironically, happiness is the only positive one.) At that point, I validate whichever emotion I'm feeling and tell myself I have every right to feel that way. Then I ask myself, "What do I want to do about it?" So I go from *validating* my feelings to taking action steps, which are then quickly followed with the question "What do I want in this moment?" or "What do I want today?" I also ask "Where do I want to be?" "Is this getting me closer to where I most want to be in life or pulling me away?" Those very simple questions help me get back on track. It's not just a matter of sitting, thinking, and theorizing about it. I actually work to put into motion the change I want to take place.

Another technique that helps is to write things down. It's true that when you write things down you're much clearer. It also helps me go from my wants to what my action plan is to get those wants. I'll simplify it by noting which two or three things I want to do towards where I want to be *today* – in other words, prioritizing. Otherwise I'll try to do everything and paralyze myself.

Chambers:

As a success coach, what do you find that most people are unfamiliar with about your industry?

Kirch:

What most people don't know is that the most important thing in this industry is building relationships. It's not about an end destination, but more of a matter of diving into the most important relationship you will ever have which is the relationship with yourself. We often focus on external relationships and forego our internal relationship which is the most important in life. My job as a success coach and counselor is to help in building that internal relationship and help you to identify what it is that you want to do, and most importantly, who you want to be while you're doing what you're doing. It's for me to ask all the right questions so you can come up with all your best answers. It's not simply about *telling* people what to do or creating a timeline or strategy, although these can be very useful tools in the process.

As a success coach the most important thing I start with is asking simple questions. They help to identify what is holding people back and preventing them from achieving success, pursuing their passions and receiving their wants. The questions also help in the development process of that one most important relationship which is the relationship with self.

Success coaching is a gift, a craft, an art, just like any other creative undertaking. It's a beautiful flowing relationship between coach and client, whether one-on-one or in a group setting. The larger group setting requires people to not only learn to build internal relationships but being able to connect with others where everyone is helping to bring each other to that "Aha" moment. This, in turn, helps to move them forward and begin to come from an abundance place of passion and *want* which positions them to do amazing things. As Emerson noted, "Nothing great was ever accomplished without enthusiasm."

Chambers:

How do you define failure and what do you feel keeps people from seeing sunshine when it's doomsday?

Kirch:

I define failure as being stuck in what appears to be failure. It's not necessarily mistakes that are failures but it's turning your back on your own best self that is failure. It's giving up on your dreams; it's settling for mediocrity. It's settling into what is convenient or easy because fear leads instead of passion leading. Failure and judgment – judgment from others and judgment of themselves – causes people to quit going after what they really want in life. They quit being who they really are. What is perceived as failure is actually opportunity. It's an opportunity to learn from the feedback that failure provides. However, if you stay stuck and never move forward and do not take advantage of those lessons, then you have failed. Failure causes people to live primarily from a fear perspective and not a perspective of love and passion. And failure causes poeple to live in the past, rather than in the present.

Chambers:

What's the difference between giving up and actually failing at something? Or is there a difference?

Kirch:

Giving up is turning your back on your best self. It's forgetting who you are. For me, it's cutting myself off from my Creator who loves me unconditionally and even though my Creator is always connected to me, I feel separated when I have given up on me or have forgotten who I am. Giving up is buying into the idea that you're not meant to be incredible or amazing or help others to do the same.

On the other hand failing is a temporary state. It's an opportunity to learn and actually get closer to your goal. It can be feedback instead of just an endpoint that you cannot move past. It's that "Yeah, I made a mistake and that's okay." For example, it takes the average child 300 times to fall before learning to walk. Kids don't quit after falling down…they keep getting up, learning from each time they fall down. It's the idea of failing forward; it's a forward motion instead of something that prevents motion.

The difference between giving up and failing is opportunity. Giving up is turning your back on yourself whereas failing is taking the opportunity to learn and grow from mistakes or missteps. This goes back to where I want to have the best relationship I can with myself. The only way I can do that is to love me unconditionally, accepting all of my feelings and failures *even when I am awful* in terms of being a mom, a wife, a success coach, or a counselor. I mess up and I do at times come from deficit. My goal is to realize it, recognize it and move forward much quicker than before when I would get stuck. Everyday that I get out of it more quickly, I am living that much more as the person I want to be.

Chambers:
So is it like a muscle where as you continue to practice it and practice it you'll continue to quickly realize it and move forward faster and more efficiently?

Kirch:
Absolutely!

Chambers:
How do you channel fear into productivity?

Kirch:
I focus on the action of what I want rather than the inaction that results in what I don't want. I'm intentional about how I feel, similar to the whole idea of feeling the fear and doing it any way. I apply that principle not just to my fears, but also when I'm sad, angry, hurt or

any other feelings. I also validate that I have a right to feel the way that I do and then ask myself what I want to do now that I'm aware of my feelings. If for some reason I'm holding on to those feelings and it's serving me to do so, I'm okay with that. However, I do know that holding onto negative feelings does not serve an overall purpose. The sooner we recognize how we feel to the fullest extent then we can let it go. Otherwise denying feelings or pushing them down causes an iceberg effect that directs thoughts, feelings, and actions. Once the feelings are released it's time to decide what you want to do in order to get closer to where you want to be. So I'll say something like, "When I think about doing something I've never done before, I feel scared....I have every right to feel scared." Then, I'll ask myself, "Am I ready to let go of feeling scared and focus on the action step that will bring me closer to what I want?" If I'm not ready, I don't rush it, but usually I don't choose to hold onto feeling scared for too long... it doesn't serve me.

Other things that help me channel fear are having mentors, coaches, friends and family to hold me accountable and validate my feelings. The external validation is not the most important part however I am an external validation "junky" and it still helps for others to say, "Yes, you have every right to feel that way." Having unconditional support is huge in terms of getting over fears because on the days when I don't believe in myself, my supporters believe in me. I have a network of people that I call on for different things. Over the years, I've learned who can help me with what I need at the time that I need it. For example, sometimes I need a kick in the butt, so I have one friend that I call for that. Other times I have somebody that I just want to be my cheerleader and tell me they love me no matter what–I have more than one person for that. And there are times that require a mix of both kicker and cheerleader and other times where I just need help thinking through where it is I want to be.

As a counselor and success coach what most helps me get through fear are other people. I am very intentional regarding the type of energy I surround myself with. This is huge for me in terms of connecting and establishing relationships with other people who are like-minded. If the people within the network are not like-minded, they can suck you down into a rabbit hole with them to commiserate and be negative – this can turn into a negative "feeding frenzy". In the classroom, I have experienced this type of negative feeding with my students. For example, I may ask someone how their weekend was, and they may respond with how awful it was and share the story. Then another student will chime in and add to the story stating how awful their weekend was. All of a sudden you have a vortex of negative energy bouncing off the walls from one student to the next, everyone trying to "one-down" (rather than "one-up") each other on how bad their weekend was, as if they'll get a prize for having the worst experience. My response is certainly not to be impressed by how awful their life is. Neither is my response a simple "Okay, let's move on." Instead, I ask how what happened made them *feel*. Once they've shared their feelings–whether sad, angry, hurt, etc., I then ask "How long would you like me to help you support your feelings in that?" This is not a loaded question, or a question with a hidden agenda or sarcasm attached. I honestly want to help others to feel whatever they are feeling for however long they want or need to feel it. It's only then that we can let feelings go and move on! Most times once the negative feelings have an opportunity to be voiced and felt, most people get off the "negative train" pretty quickly, and make a decision to move on in the direction of where they want to be.

This highlights an interesting point. Whenever you ask people what they are afraid of, most often the response is "I'm not afraid." Really? I'm scared of a lot of things. I *feel* (not "stuff," not ignore, not deny) the fear and do it anyway. Denying how we feel – including the feeling of fear–gets us into trouble. When we deny how we feel, it festers, and it leads our thoughts and actions blindly, where we have no control. When we bring our feelings and fears into the light, we have the opportunity to do something about them. So to answer your question of how I channel fear into productivity, I recognize it and then flip it on its head.

You've probably heard the acronym for F.E.A.R–"False Evidence Appearing Real,"–I agree with this assessment and believe that fear is the worst possible use of imagination. Flipping all of those mental constructs on their head is just as easy. Instead you could think of F.E.A.R as Fantastic Expectations Appearing Real.

To sum it up, I flip everything on its head when thoughts are going down a negative road. I recognize it, feel it, validate my feelings, and then determine what I want to do that will lead me to where I want to be, experiencing what I want to feel.

Chambers:

Would you recommend others create a board of directors for their life?

Kirch:

Absolutely! It goes back to being a true leader. For me, the big thing about being a leader, being successful or being happy is recognizing when I need help. This, I think is one of the most important things we can do in life – one of our most important life skills. Yet so many people choose not to do one of the most important things we can do for ourselves. We don't ask–not even simply because of past experiences, but because many of us were taught, programmed, and socialized specifically *not* to ask for help. Here come the "should/need/have to" statements. "I should be perfect." "I need to be perfect for others to love me." "I have to do this by myself." And then there are those who don't ask for help because of the treatment they received from parents, teachers, counselors or whomever. Unfortunately, too often those we turn to for help early in life, shame us for asking. These bad experiences helped shape our thoughts surrounding asking for help, not realizing those individuals were coming from a place of deficit.

It also may be perceived that those who ask for help are weak and should be capable of doing it themselves. Asking for help is actually a sign of strength and wisdom because you are recognizing what you know and what you don't know, and thus seeking resources to fill in those gaps.

Chambers:

Is a way of giving back being the type of person whom you would seek for help?

Kirch:

Yes, I'm always looking for ways to ensure the personal interaction between me and another person is a win-win for both of us. It's my way of giving back based on what I have received.

If I can help others come from a place of abundance by giving of myself, it's a boomerang effect. The more love, energy, and optimism that I give to others, the more I get in return. I don't have to wonder whether I'm going to get it back in return because I believe in a world where you get what you put out.

So if I put out positive energy, I get positive energy back. Anyone can experience this boomerang effect by simple going out and smiling at, say, twenty people. See what you get in return. This is a simple example that shows what you can get if you put this principle into action everyday. You'll see what you put out there comes back to you one hundred fold.

Chambers:

What was your greatest "Aha" moment in business?

Kirch:

My biggest "Aha" moment in business was when I learned that I am absolutely capable of doing amazing things in business because it's about relationship building. And that's everything that I'm about. Growing up, I learned to see business was about making money, the bottom line, what you could get, and how to deceive people so profits could be made–which are all unfortunate myths. What *is* true is that somebody doesn't have to lose in order for someone else to win! So a big "Aha" for me was when I learned that what I bring to business is my amazing ability to create relationships and bring people to what they want, creating a win-win. That's what business, life, and education is all about. It's creating a situation where everyone comes from an abundance place.

Chambers:

What type of strategies do you use to fight time management?

Kirch:

First of all, I'm very intentional with my words so I wouldn't even say that I "fight" time management, because I believe in that idea of what you resist persists. So I don't try to fight time management. If I'm fighting it, then it's something I really don't *want* to do. Instead of thinking of time management as this beast, I break it up into pieces using my wants as a prioritizing factor. I write down my wants and prioritize them based on things I want this year, this week, this day – thereby, forming a "to do" list. I then cross off everything but the top 20-25% of the list – based on *when* I want it and its order of importance. The way I determine what to cross of the list is I ask myself "Is this helping me get closer to my *biggest* wants, dreams, and passions?" Once I have my list narrowed down, I focus on those few things and work to do them really, really well. Being this intentional gives me the freedom to not be perfect in everything because my focus has shifted to specific things and not everything.

Right now, my intentionality is to be really amazing, happy, and successful in whatever I choose to spend time doing – whether it's with my husband, my sons, my students, or even strangers. Life is much simpler when you can focus on the things you want and not force yourself into things based on obligations or "shoulds." If I wake up and say I have to go to work, I check myself and I say, "What do I want to do?" The reality is that many times, I actually want to go to work. However, we have been so programmed to say we *have* to do things–like going to work–that even when we want to do things, we don't embrace it. Saying "I have to" is implicit negativity and it's setting ourselves up for failure. When it comes to things like the "daily business of living" kinds of things, like doing the laundry or going to the market, I think about why I *want* to do them. I *want* to do the laundry because I want clean clothes to wear, or I *want* to go to the market because I want to eat healthy food. Then, even the "daily business of living things" becomes something we want to do, rather than have to do or should do.

Chambers:

As a success coach, when someone is down and frustrated how can you help them focus on the positive versus the negative?

Kirch:

It goes back to asking different questions like, "When do you feel most perfectly you? In a perfect world what would you be doing?" Many times, I get a lot of resistance because so often people think they shouldn't go for their dreams or they don't believe it's really possible. Being stuck in a place of fear causes you to ask troublesome questions like "What happens if I fail?" As their coach and counselor, I'll keep asking the same question in different ways. I may ask, "What inspires you? When do you feel so alive that you are on a natural high?" I may have them do an exercise where I suggest they paint a picture of themselves in their mind in which they are completely fulfilled and joyful. I'll then ask what they are doing in the picture. Another question I may ask is "In a perfect world, if you knew you could not fail what would you be doing?" Usually after enough questions, I'll see a spark in their eyes and that's when we've identified those lost dreams and passions. I let them know I feel an energy shift. In this moment I want them to begin to recognize they are perfectly themselves coming from abundance instead of deficit and fear. The energy shift leads to a floodgate of hopes, dreams, and possibilities. Now if for some reason they are answering the questions, but I'm not seeing a spark or feeling an energy shift, I'll speak to that. I'll say things like, "You are saying things, but I don't see anything in your non-verbal language indicating these are your true wants." I'll ask, "Is this really what you want?" Many times, in response, people will say "No, it's what my parents want for me," or "it's what my spouse wants for me." Or they may say, "I don't even know what I want because I have never really thought about it." Oftentimes, these words are accompanied with intense emotion – this validates that we're getting to the heart of the matter. Remembering who they really are and beginning to believe again in the possibility of pursuing and attaining dreams can be very emotional. They begin thinking and feeling about who they are and who they want to be. This is a big starting point in terms of self discovery. So as a success coach, a bulk of my job is asking all the right questions, helping people to think about their lives and who they are. Inspiring those thoughts helps them come up with their own best answers.

Chambers:

What advice and encouragement would you give to a budding entrepreneur?

Kirch:

First determine what you most want. Then write it down and say it out loud often. Clarifying your wants, writing them down, and verbalizing them are very effective tools in actualizing your dreams. Share your wants with your support network, being sure not to disclose them with those who will be naysayer of your dreams. Because everything is about feelings, I would also add a visualization/feeling exercise. Identify what feelings you expect to feel when you attain your dream or goal, and then actually put yourself in that moment and feel those feelings as if you've already completed your dream. For example, I would say in my own life that when I see my books in Barnes and Noble with the New York Times best selling tag, when I picture that moment, I know that I'll *feel* amazing, happy, blessed and even more inspired to help others go after their dreams. Instead of imagining what will happen if I fail, I'm using my imagination positively, putting myself in that moment of success. Feeling – even before it's happened–what it's like to see your ultimate wants realized helps to push us forward towards our goals and dreams. I encourage people to intentionally identify their wants, and I also encourage seeking out a mentor who will help guide them to where they want to be.

And lastly something that absolutely helps me is the power of "Thank-you's." Regardless of your passion, whether it's related to education, business, or being an entrepreneur, it is important to thank those who have already helped, those you are currently helping, and those who will help in the future. Whether they are currently in your life or on the way, the ability to express gratitude keeps you in a positive abundance mindset, and more importantly, "feeling set." It's very difficult to remain in deficit when you're saying thank you.

Chambers:

What inspires you?

Kirch:

I am inspired by anyone who is confidently walking in the direction of his dreams even if he is scared stiff while doing so. I am inspired by anyone who is amazingly and beautifully her true self and lives her truth no matter what the circumstances are. Anyone who has the ability to laugh at herself, take risks, and comes from love and passion–even in the face of fear–are all inspirations to me.

Chambers:

What inspired you to become a success coach?

Kirch:

The crappy coaches, counselors, and teachers that I had in the past who belittled my dreams–out of their deficit–which spilled over to me inspired me to do things differently. And then I've had the blessing of having many coaches, teachers, and counselors who have been the opposite of that–lifting me up. They believed in me and helped me to do things that I didn't think I was capable of doing. Their pushing and challenging me, being critics with love so that I could move forward and get out of my safety zone–all these things helped to inspire me to want more.

I'm also inspired by the opportunity to help others and the feeling I get from being a blip on other peoples journeys as they're rediscovering, relearning, remembering who they really are.

Chambers:

What is the greatest reward of being a success coach?

Kirch:

The greatest reward is being a part of someone else's journey. I get to be a part of someone else's life as they work towards being their best self coming from joy and passion. The feeling that I get from being instrumental in helping others make their dreams come true is like no other. I know I'm good at what I do and I get external validation, however, the internal rush I get when I see the smiles on their faces, when I see the light bulb go on, when I see them filled up because in this moment they are realizing who they are meant to be is more than enough validation. And then to see them walking in the direction of hopes, dreams, and passion…I get really emotional about it because of that soul-to-soul connection. It's a connection on a deeper level…something that is bigger than this earth.

Chambers:

What is the greatest risk you've ever taken and was it worth it?

Kirch:

That is a really hard question because there are lots of risks that I feel I've taken. Giving up a Division 1 scholarship and transferring to a school that was a better fit for me was a risk. Going for my lifeguard certification, sky diving, applying to grad school, signing up and completing two marathons all were risks. Starting anything new – playing the guitar, starting pilates and yoga, volunteering have all been risks. Making a life-long commitment to my husband, deciding to have children, buying a home were all risks. The wonderful thing I have experienced in the last couple of years is the more risks I take, the more risk I am willing to take, and the more rewards I experience. So every risk I've ever taken has absolutely been worth it!

Chambers:

If you could do anything and you knew you would not fail what would you do?

Kirch:

I would continue to do what I'm doing. I would continue being a counselor and a success coach helping others dreams come true. I would continue to work with college athletes and would expand to professional athletes, as well. I would travel and expand the people that I work with by writing more, and having the opportunity to be a coach to an even broader audience. I would travel more extensively in terms of speaking engagements and eventually around the world. I'm especially drawn towards people in the world who are most in deficit, who are in the worst of circumstances, who at first glance appear to be hopeless–so I would go to those places around the world and do everything I could to restore hope, dreams, and passion.

Chambers:
If you could share any advice with someone what would it be?

Kirch:

Something that is very important to me is giving credit where credit is due. So if I could share any words, the words I would choose to share are something my friend Nina Privitt taught our family, which is "You are valuable, you are capable and thus you are responsible."

Stacy Kirch
Counselor

2701 Fairview Road
Costa Mesa, CA 92626

powerwithstacy@me.com
www.powerwithtshirts.com
www.powerwithparenting.com

Chapter 9

Stephanie Landers
Real Estate Invester/Coach

David E. Chambers (Chambers):
You had a very unique childhood. You were born in a German labor camp during WWII. Can you explain to us what that was like?

Stephanie Landers (Landers):
I don't actually remember the labor camp. I can tell you what my parents have told me. My father had two children to feed, and he became a cook in the camp. That's how he managed to feed us, and take care of us. Other than that, I don't have any remembrance of the labor camp at all. I do remember being an airport sometime lat-

er, because my mother's voice echoed when she spoke to me. My youngest sister, who is a year or two younger than me, was hungry and crying, and I heard the echoes of her cries. That's about all I remember about that period.

Chambers:

How did your family come to the United States from Ukraine?

Landers:

The Germans took Ukrainians, like my parents, to Germany, and my great uncle sponsored us to come to the U.S. and gave us a place to live in Yonkers, New York.

Chambers:

How did your family find work when they came to the Unites States?

Landers:

My great uncle found my father a job of some sort after we arrived. Later my father worked for the New York Central Railroad as a cleaner who cleaned trains at night. Subsequently, after being at the railroad for a number of months, he was in a work-related accident, and did not work for ten years after that. He had surgery-after-surgery, and my mother had to support us for those years. Neither of my parents spoke any English. The Ukrainian Catholic Church in Yonkers put me into school so that I could learn English and help my parents learn to speak English.

Chambers:

At a young age you must have learned how to overcome obstacles. From those tough experiences, have you found tools and techniques to over-come challenges in the business world?

Landers:

I overcame my obstacles because I have a strong sense of awareness, a strong sense of what's right, and a strong spiritual sense that I am always being guided, cared for, and provided for. I was able to get a great education, which is the key to my success in the business world. I never stop learning.

Chambers:

When people are down and are having a tough time, what recommendations would give to help them overcome their obstacles?

Landers:

There are a few things...One of the things I would point out is that everything starts in the mind, and we must control our thoughts. It's very easy, when things are going badly, to ruminate in your mind, continually going over the bad things that are happening or things that have happened to you in the past. The way I function in such situations is by reframing everything in my mind. If a negative thought arises, I reframe it so that it's positive. I may reframe the incident, the person, or the way I respond to that particular problem, so that it doesn't have any negative charge inside my body.

Chambers:

Many times people in the business world get stuck in a mode of fear. What do you do to channel or overcome your fear?

Landers:

In the real estate world, a lot of things can and do go wrong—testing your patience and endurance. One of the things I tell myself is *to lighten up.* I have a tendency to take everything very seriously, so I tell myself to lighten up.

The next thing I do is to ask myself, "What's the worst thing that can happen?" When I ask myself that question, I go through the scenario, beginning with writing the question down, or asking it in my head. If the worst thing that can happen is that closing the deal doesn't happen, say, for two weeks, well, that's not a terrible thing. That's actually a gift because it gives us time to straighten out anything that needs to be straightened. It also allows me time to get clarity.

One of the things that happens to you when things seem to be going badly, is that you feel it in your physical body. When I feel it in my body, I know it's about fear, and I know it's about money and my feelings about money. It is very difficult to rid your body of that fear. What I do is to actually feel myself step to the side. So, I'll look at the problem straight on, and then I take a sidestep in my mind. This allows me to look at the problem from a different angle, and it releases the binding of fear inside my body.

Chambers:

You've channeled your energy and overcome your fear, you've become a leader in the real estate world to be a successful entrepreneur. What does it take to become a great leader?

Landers:

For me, there is a spiritual component to leadership. I believe in grace, trust grace, believe in God, and trust myself.

Chambers:

How do you define success?

Landers:

I have to say I categorize success in several ways. What kind of person am I? Am I successful internally? Do I feel in alignment with myself? And the people I'm working with in the real estate world?

When I look at my terms of success, I look at what I accomplished 'til now. What my strengths are, what I have achieved. Am I happy. Have I amde a positive impact on people I care about. Have I helped others find future success.

Chambers:

What inspired you to get into real estate?

Landers:

I love every house that I see. I see potential in every house. I can see exactly what it could be, even if the walls are falling down or the place needs $50,000 in work. I can see the potential.

Chambers:

Your passion for real estate is obvious. How old were you when you discovered that passion?

Landers:

My passion for real estate started when I was eighteen-years-old. We were an immigrant, low-income family; my father and mother began looking at houses about five miles from where we were living. One day my father asked me, "How would you like it if we bought this house?" It was twenty-thousand dollars, and I thought that was tons of money. Ultimately, he bought a house that he was going to rehab, and I was involved with all the projects of revamping that house. It was a very, very, old house—it hardly had any plumbing, and didn't even have a bathroom. I helped with every aspect from the flooring, paneling and window treatments to the kitchen. The reason why I helped was because my mom was ill in the hospital. I helped so that when she came home, she had a home to come to. After helping him on that first house, from then on, every time I saw a house, I saw it in a different way—differently from everyone else.

Fast forward to after I'd gotten married, and my husband and I bought a house to rehab, as well. Our second house, we bought new. Those two instances of rehabbing a house, and then having a new house, instilled in me a love and passion for homes. One of the reasons for this, I think, is that we lived so poor and were in a tenement right by the train tracks. Interestingly enough, we didn't know we were poor, but the children at school told us that we were.

Chambers:

I know your father and mother have been great mentors to you. What other mentors have you known who've had a major influence on you?

Landers:

When I was taking a shorthand class in high school, my tenth grade teacher mentored me. What's interesting is that I was failing shorthand, but he believed in me, and I graduated high school with high honors. He saw the potential of me entering the business world. He helped me with the applications for Berkeley, and not only did I get in, but I got a scholarship. So, he was my first mentor and helped me transition into the adult world.

Chambers:
What should a person look for when they are trying to find a mentor?

Landers:
A connection. When I found a mentor, what I learned is that there was a connection which I felt on an internal level. I knew that no matter what, I had to work with this person. In my head, all I could hear was all the obstacles, but my heart and intuition were telling me, "You must do this."

What I had to do was to get my head and my heart to talk, and to find a reason for my head to say yes. I found that reason and I ended up working with this mentor for several months. He changed my life.

So, to answer your question, I think you have to feel it on an internal level. The mind doesn't always tell you exactly what's right because the mind can be very fearful. If you go inward, into your heart, you'll always do the right thing. You always know what's right for you. You will find a way.

Chambers:
With your expertise in business, what techniques have you seen that make a great mentor?

Landers:
A mentor has to be able to listen and pick out the gems that the person they're working with has inside of them. A great mentor has to

be able to draw those out. To me, the internal is more important than the external. The spiritual is more important than the physical. We could have money falling out of the sky, but if we're not able to financially enjoy it. If we're not able to properly use the money, if we don't feel grateful, if we don't feel like we deserve it, what good is money? We need to be internally balanced first, before we can feel like we deserve the financial success, because we deserve it. But parts of us, which come from our religious training or our background (parents, teachers) can create within us a faulty blueprint for what money really means. We need to get that straightened out first before we can even realize that we deserve money, and that money *should* come to us.

Chambers:

Being as busy and successful as you are, what techniques do you use to help you with time management?

Landers:

Time management is so important. One of the things I do is prioritize my day. I actually categorize it into personal, physical, spiritual, nutritional, and business activities. I take time off for myself every single morning to say I'm grateful for my day. That seems to put everything into place for me. I spend a half-hour looking at e-mails and answering them quickly, and then I return my phone calls. This way I know who needs what, and when. I also find out if there are any clients in distress who I need to take care of. If I communicate with them in the morning, they don't have to be distressed all day long. Then I keep my appointments. I put them off until between 11:00 and 3:00 in the daytime so that I have everything organized in the morning. That's generally how I work.

Chambers:

What advice would you give to someone who wants to get into real estate and wants to be an entrepreneur?

Landers:

The common thread among the entrepreneurs I know is that they have a burning desire to *be* entrepreneurs. They have this feeling that they just have to do it, no matter what. Then if they decide that they want to be entrepreneurs in real estate, one of the things they need to decide is if they want to be a real estate agent.

It is not necessary to be a real estate agent in order to be a real estate entrepreneur. What I would suggest to anyone is to really decide how they want their world to look, and how they will get there. *What is the process?* If real estate is part of that, what do they want to be? A real estate investor. If so, what kind of real estate investor? Do they want to purchase residential properties? Commercial properties? Do they have the income to support their own ventures? Do they have the education? If they don't have the income, and they don't have the education, then I would suggest that they get the education by becoming a student of real estate and learning everything they possibly can. Knowledge is power.

Chambers:

What inspires you?

Landers:

Just hearing that question beings tears to my eyes... I always feel like I have God on my side. Usually I call it the universe or the spiritual component of the universe.

I get inspired by books. I get inspired by a great sunset. I feel like I am the luckiest person in the world because internally, spiritually, I have always endeavored to be the best that I could be. I feel like I am one with the universe, and the universe sends me to places and people, or sends people to me—something that will touch my heart. I always go inside, and ask if something is right for me; if a person is right for me; if a decision is right for me, and I always ask my heart. In my heart resides all the answers.

Chambers:
What has been the greatest "Ah-ha" moment in business for you?

Landers:
I can tell you that it is never as tough as you think it is. Ah-ha. It is easier than I ever thought it would be. Ah-ha. All I had to do was take the first step. Ah-ha. Everything else falls into place after that. I never knew that...

Chambers:
What is the greatest risk you've ever taken, and was it worth it?

Landers:
The greatest risk that comes to mind was deciding to go to massage therapy school when my children were young. I left all my friends and my family. I lived in Connecticut for a year-and-a-half. It was very scary. I'd been in a protected environment while living with my husband, my children, and my family. I went into a world where there were different colors, different cultures, and all different types of people.

In massage school I actually started to become who I was meant to be. The risk was worth it. I found out who I was. I found out what I was capable of, and I expanded my world. Every person who I met, I knew I could touch. I don't mean massaging their necks, or touching their shoulders. I mean I could touch them in some way because I could meet them on a level where they knew they were safe with me. I was maybe thirty-nine years-old then; from that time until my age now—I'm sixty-two—that's been my foundation. It's been a very healthy foundation in many, many ways.

Chambers:
If you could share any advice with someone, what would it be?

Landers:
I think we should trust ourselves. As a woman, I know that we must trust ourselves and believe in ourselves. I don't think people do this. I think that they look for empowerment outside of themselves, and they just have to look inside of themselves. They look for happiness outside themselves before they become whole inside.

Another piece of advice would be for people to mentor themselves. We all look for mentors, and they are out there. They're teachers, they're friends, and they're business people. There are all types of mentors, but we don't always see them. We don't always meet them right away, so while we're trying to learn, and while we're looking for that mentor, we can mentor ourselves. There are probably hundreds of books in bookstores, friend's houses, and libraries; in every one of those books is a mentor. There are writers and stories about people who have been very successful—inspiring stories from all the way back. There is the Bible. Every one of those books, every one of those stories, on every single page, there is a word, thought, idea, or statement that could help mentor you. That is what I do.

Chambers:
What do you want your legacy to be?

Landers:
I have been talking about legacy for the past three days. For some reason it has been on my mind. I always speak about legacy in terms of my children. What kind of a legacy, as a mother, could I give my children? I've always thought, from the day they were born, about their legacy, what kind of people they would become, and what kind of person I was to become as a mother.

My legacy is that I've tried the very best that I could in every single circumstance that was presented to me in my life, and I did not fail myself. I have been proud of myself. I have been proud of the way I raised my children. My sons have become adults—successful adults, and incredible human beings. In terms of my legacy to my children, they will know that I was the best that I could be.

Stephanie Landers
ANKA Enterprises
Conversations with Entrepreneurs

113618 N 99th Ave. #803
Sun City, AZ 85351

Chapter 10

Sara McKay

Personal Trainer

David E. Chambers (Chambers):
As a Success Coach, what have you seen in helping people to become
better leaders in their line of work?

Sara McKay (McKay):
I've helped people achieve more confidence in themselves, and the
choices that they make. People who become self-motivated, want
more and I help them find that drive within themselves. People who
are open-minded individuals, people who never believed in them-
selves or their abilities change. You can see it in everything they do;

it's especially noticeable in how they carry themselves; their walk, their posture, their head is now held high. They speak with more confidence because their proud of themselves and what they've accomplished.

Chambers:

As you're talking about self-motivation, how do you feel people get self-motivated?

McKay:

One of the first things that I do to help get someone self motivated is determine what is needed to achieve their goals. Together we look at their workouts, not just one workout at a time but instead weeks in advance.

Then I give them homework, something that they are responsible for themselves. This holds them accountable for their own success, this helps them realize that they don't really need me to achieve their goals; it's all up to them. Truly, they do the work; I'm just the one that guides them in the right direction. They start to realize that it's up to them to be self-motivated; to get out of bed in the morning to do their cardio; or instead of staying on the couch for the weekend they choose to play tennis or go for a hike. These are the types of choices that help make these types of activities a habit.

Chambers:

So, what this sounds like is, "Accountability is what allows someone to succeed."

McKay:

Yes!

Chambers:

Let's talk about accountability – for people to reach their goals, do you find that it's more empowering for them to have a mentor, and an accountability coach? Or do you find that people can do it on their own?

McKay:

No, I believe people definitely need an accountability coach and a mentor in every way, shape, or form... absolutely! I mean, honestly, most people need it long-term for their business, for their personal goal, for their relationships.

Chambers:

If someone wants to find a mentor, or an accountability coach, what process should they go through? What should they look for in an accountability coach, or a success coach?

McKay:

I think, to find the right success coach, they need to find someone that inspires them to be better, someone that they admire and look up to, someone that they wish that they would be more like. This would give them more of an indication that they've found the mentor that is best for them.

Chambers:

What makes one coach better than another?

McKay:

In my opinion if you can see that he/she is living the lifestyle that they're trying to coach you on then you've found a right match. In my line of work there are a lot of trainers who don't look or act the part. It's always better to find someone who is in better shape them you are. Someone who lives a healthy lifestyle, someone who you really have admiration for.

Chambers:

So, what made you decide to want to get into physical fitness and want to be a success coach for the mind, body and soul?

McKay:

I've been physically active my entire life, and I have a great love for sports. When I was in college, I was very interested and involved in weight training. In college I was on the track team, this gave me visibility to other athletes. I was a smaller sized girl in her teens who was visibly stronger than most. I was able to sprint and run, and then go play tennis for four hours, and I'd be fine.

Pretty soon I was approached by football players, wrestlers and other athletes in the gym, all looking for advice on which weights to use and how often. I started helping others and I loved it, and finally someone said, "Hey! Have you ever thought about being a coach or a trainer?" and I was like "Not really."

At that time I was so into my own athletics, that it wasn't something I had ever thought seriously about. Eventually people started asking if they could pay me to workout and train them! I said, "No, no! I'll just help you" and finally, when trying to decide what to do after college I thought "Hey I can get paid for this?! Sweet!"

Ever since then, it just stuck. After a few years in both Portland and Seattle I decided that if I wanted to become a better trainer I needed to move to California, to meet trainers who were better than

I was, so that I could improve my skills and be challenged.

Chambers:

As you were successful in college in your athletic career, you had a tragedy that changed the way you looked at sports and medicine. What happened, and how did you overcome your tragedy?

McKay:

I had a track scholarship in college, but most of my focus was on training. Unfortunately, I over-trained and one day in javelin practice, I tore my pectoral muscle, and was out, and lost my track scholarship. I was really upset and decided to leave school my junior year.

I decided that I loved weight training and I was really good at it, and that led to me becoming a personal trainer. I've had the opportunity to do this for the last six years and have been fortunate enough to be successful at it.

When I started my athletics in college, I also started competing in body building and fitness competitions. I've been doing this for the last 10 years; and now I'm also a judge for various Bodybuilding and Fitness Competitions. I'm able to help other women and men achieve their goals in the sport. It's very rewarding.

Chambers:

Wonderful! Getting to be a part of Gold's in Venice… it truly is an honor. How did that come about, and how did you take advantage of that opportunity?

McKay:

Actually someone who knew me, when I was a trainer in Oregon, was working for Gold's and he found out that I was living up in Seattle. He got a hold of me, and asked, "Have you ever thought about training down here, in Gold's?" And I said, "Absolutely! But I just never thought it was possible." And he said, "Well, it's very much possible. We'd like to have you. Are you interested?" I said "Yes." My best friend had already been living down here at the time. So, it was the perfect timing for me to move down here and live with her.

Chambers:

What do you attribute your success to?

McKay:

I would say my dedication and accountability. My clients know that without a doubt, they can count on me; I'm here, whenever they need me. I never cancel, I give them a hundred percent of attention and do whatever it takes to help them reach their goals.

Chambers:

So, when people aren't accountable for themselves – I'm sure you run into this as a success coach – how do you inspire them to get back on point?

McKay:

I often find that it's much more than just about the weight-loss. A lot of the time this leads to conversations about other things going on in their lives. They feel that I'm the person that they can talk to, about relationships, family, or whatever.

I inspire them by getting them to feel more comfortable with our relationship. I tell them "Look... I have family and friends that have been in your boat, and believe me, I'm here to help you along the way.

You're going to have ups and downs, just like anything you're trying to accomplish, but I'm going to be here for you, through the entire process, until you reach that goal." I'm really good at listening to my clients and they know I care. And so, that helps inspire them to be better within themselves.

Chambers:

So, if someone has a goal, and if someone is going for it, and they get derailed, how can you help them get that focus back in, to go where they really want to be?

McKay:

I try to help them by mapping out a goal for them, one day at a time. I help them with their time management, and show them that there is time for them to set aside for themselves, and that usually leads to their success.

Chambers:

So, do you find that for most people, when they get derailed, it's a matter of time management and focus of their true goals?

McKay:

Absolutely! I believe that when most people get derailed and loose sight of their goal, they end up putting other things first.

What I usually do is sit down with them and figure out what exactly they're doing in the day. Whether it's their children, school, driving around, meetings, work, whatever it is. We look at their schedule and I show them that "Yes, you do have twenty minutes in this day to set aside for yourself."

And then I help them, and show them what to do and how to spend that time. Even if it's only 20 minutes, they're still going forward and reaching their goal. It doesn't mean they have to spend an hour; if they can do twenty minutes everyday, sooner or later, they will reach their goal.

Chambers:

As a weight trainer, competitor, judge, and strategist... how have you personally stayed focused for so many years?

McKay:

For the most part, weight-training and staying active is what has helped with my own personal stress. It's what I strive for and what I've always worked towards. Sometimes, when I get off-course, I just refocus and I think about people who motivate me within the gym, or other people that I've seen. I know that I have been in that same place before.

I'll sit down and rewrite my goals, and give myself time to just re-group and get back on track. And within less than 24 hours, no matter what has happened, I feel amazing again... every time.

Chambers:

In business, in relationships, in physical health... no matter what people are trying to achieve, they need to have a goal. So, how do you help to write down goals, and stay focused on their goals?

McKay:

My clients typically have something specific their goals are tied to. A wedding, a vacation, a specific weight they are trying to reach or even if it's just 20 lbs that they're trying to lose. We sit down and write every single goal that they have, and I know that there's always more than just that one so I break it down.

"Okay, what brought you to 20 lbs? There's more than that." "What's going to help you get there?" "Do you have any injuries?" And then, with that, we figure out the long-term goals: "Okay, it's going to take you six months." And that's a long goal. They think, "Okay! That's six months from now."

So then, we break it down – a month at a time, and then within that month. When I'm with the client, I'll say, "Okay! Within this week..." and then I break it down further. "Today, this is what your goal is," and then, by the end of those seven days, I'm like, "Sweet! This first goal, this week... it's done. Don't even worry about it. You're there!"

We'll keep having these conversations until they reach their ultimate goal. You have to find your ultimate goal, and then you have to break it down, so that you have something to look forward to, just around the corner.

Chambers:

I really like that, because I've heard people say before, that, "We overestimate what we can do in a year, and we underestimate what we can do in a decade." And that leads to these lofty goals – "I want to be a millionaire by 30, or by 40, or by 50.""I want to do this" or "I want to be this size," or "I want to look this day." But they don't break that down and compartmentalize it to such a small area that it's obtainable. So, is that what you're advising? To make sure that if you have your goal, you break it down into so small that you can perceive it, and see it, and achieve it?

McKay:

Yes! Every time you make a goal, it still needs to be broken down even if it's a 24 hour goal. You still have to, because you have to figure out what's going to get you to the end result. It's just not that one goal – it's not that easy. It's going to take steps to get you there. And just like someone who's trying to climb that corporate ladder, or whatever their profession is, it's going to take certain steps to get there. Everything does. And so, in order to achieve that, you've got to figure out what those steps are, and then you've got to accomplish them.

Chambers:

What recommendations do you have for staying focused to those goals, when you make them small enough, and let's say you fall off the bandwagon, and you lose sight? How do we get back on track?

McKay:

Depending on how far they got off track, then I usually don't just say, "Let's wait until Monday," like most people say. I say, "You know what? Tomorrow… we need to wake focused, and we need to figure out what needs to be done to get that day completed. We need to start our day with a positive attitude."

So many people feel like, "Oh! I lost it. I have to wait until next week." They make excuses. But really, most people just need someone to tell them, "Look, we can start it the morning," or even, "We can start it this afternoon."

Most people have problems staying focused with their nutrition. That's the largest hurdle in my line of work. If nutrition is their goal, and they are having problems staying focused on that, I actually have to help them stay inspired, stay on track one meal at time.

Chambers:

Even with our nutrition, even with our goals, it really is breaking it down to such a small thing, that you can understand it, accomplish it, and therefore, you don't need to get hung up on, "Oh it's too lofty! I can't do it," or "Oh I failed! I'll quit." Is that correct?

McKay:

That is correct. And so when people feel like they've accomplished something, they feel much better. Even if it's one small goal. They feel that much better about themselves and it gives them that much more of a drive to keep on moving in the right direction.

Chambers:

In your line of work, what do people get hung up on? Is it disappointment, discouragement... what holds people back?

McKay:

I would say what holds people back the most, would be giving up on themselves so early – they feel like it's too hard, and that they're never going to reach their goal.

Chambers:

When you're training someone, and they seem like they want to give up – we've all had our goals, we've all had our desires, and we've given up at some time – how do you help that person get back to the point in focus?

McKay:

I tell them to believe in themselves, and that they can do this without a doubt. Maybe they've done it before, or not, but they can do this… and how much better they'll feel when they finish that last rep. Knowing that they did it to the best of their ability, with good form, and while feeling great? I tell them to try and stay positive.

Chambers:

Why do you think that people feel that they can't do it in life?

McKay:

I think that's because most people have been told so many times in their life that they can't do something, and so, they have that wall to get through. I think people today give out more negative energy than positive praises, which is disappointing.

Chambers:

As a trainer, are you battling a lot of people's mental blocks?

McKay:

Absolutely! I help people battle their mental blocks every day, and I have to try and help them overcome whatever it may be.

I feel like what has helped me the most in these six years is listening – if you listen to people, truly listen to them, they'll share with you what their mental blocks are. You'll be able to figure out the kind of person they are and what they feed off of. Most people work better with positive reinforcement approach than with a drill sergeant.

Chambers:

I'd agree with that, for sure! What does it take to be a good leader?

McKay:

I feel, to be a good leader, you've got to show confidence; you have to be dedicated in what you're doing; you have to have open-mindedness, and be willing to listen to people; to become an even stronger leader; and you definitely have to have self-motivation. You have to find something in you, to drive you to become better, and to show others how things need to be done.

Chambers:

How do you define success?

McKay:

Success, to me, is achieving something that I've set out to do and conquering it.

Chambers:

When times are tough, how do you stay focused?

McKay:

I stay focused by re-visiting my goals and re-writing them if necessary. I also try and hang out with people who are more positive and it seems like it doesn't take long for me to get back on track, and get focused again.

Chambers:

It sounds like goals are a crucial part of what you do. Do you ever get tired of writing goals, or feel too overwhelmed by your goals?

McKay:

I never get tired of writing my goals; I actually feel excited because every time I write my goals, I feel like at least one more new goal comes about.

Chambers:

What is the secret combination to finding success in your line of work?

McKay:

You have to find something about yourself that stands out – whether it's the way you look, the way you talk to people, how you stay focused on your clients because everyone's always watching!

Chambers:

Let's expound on that. If I understand what you're saying, you're talking about accentuating what is unique about you.

McKay:

Yes! Find something that's unique about you, and go with it... because it will be unique, and it will stand out.

Chambers:

How does somebody find what is unique? So often, people are fearful of standing out. How does someone muster the courage to embrace what is unique about them and to live it?

McKay:

Maybe it's as simple as talking to your friends and family – the people who you're not fearful of, the people that love you and trust you unconditionally... maybe, you can ask them and get more of an idea about yourself. In more cases than not they're going to say something you already thought of, about yourself, but it gives you more validation to do that, and be that person.

Chambers:
What inspired you to get into what you're doing now?

McKay:
Helping others – honestly, people all around me inspire me. All different shapes, and sizes, ethnicity, age groups... it doesn't matter. People all around me inspire me to do what I do. I love helping others and I love the look on people's faces when they achieve that goal, and I know that I'm helping guide them.

Chambers:
How do you define failure? What does failure mean to you?

McKay:
Failure is giving up on yourself without finishing your goal, or what you've set out to do. But honestly, I don't believe in the word failure. I think of it as throwing negativity in someone's mindset.

Chambers:
There is the acronym of fear: False Evidence Appearing Real. How do you channel that fear that people have, into productivity? How do you break through their fear to find success?

McKay:

I think to help people break through their fear is knowing what their fear is. Once you know what their fear is, you break it down into steps and figure out what they need to do to overcome their fear. It could have stemmed from something else, and so, you need to figure out what that is, help guide them, and give them options. And when you help people and give them options, it doesn't seem as much as a fear, as just a task that they're trying to accomplish at that point.

Chambers:

How has having a mentor helped you become successful?

McKay:

Oh goodness! A mentor has helped me become successful in more ways than one. I now wake up every morning and I am so excited to start my day. My mind is even more open than I ever thought it could be. I can tell that I'm positive about any situation, and I'm more calm... and then, when I'm more positive and calm, then no matter what decision I make, I know it's the best decision for me, at that time. And that is how having a mentor has helped me, and it's also opened up many, many doors that I never thought possible, that are just coming at me, left and right. It's very exciting!

Chambers:

When someone is trying to find a mentor, what should they look for?

McKay:

When someone is trying to find a mentor, they need to look for someone who has a good name in the community, who a majority of people trust and like what they're doing – they may not know them as a person, but like what they're doing for the community and for others; someone who has been involved in different organizations maybe it's big or small, it doesn't matter; someone who inspires you... again, that word is just incredible! Yes, you need to look for someone who inspires you to be a better person, and believe in yourself.

Chambers:

What has been one of your greatest A-ha moments in your line of work?

McKay:

One of my greatest A-ha moments was when my client told me that they never have to take back-pain medicine ever again, and that they can get out of bed, without help.

Chambers:

What has been one of your A-ha moments in business itself – looking at your business, looking at how you became successful as a physical trainer... what was one of those moments when you realized, "Wow! This is what I was meant to do?"

McKay:

One of my biggest A-ha moments in my success as a fitness trainer and coach is when I've been told by my clients and their friends that I have changed their life for now, and forever, and that I have taught them to love themselves again and to appreciate the body that they were given.

Chambers:

What strategies do you use to work with time management, or to stay focused on your time?

McKay:

Time management skills are things that I use to keep myself on track. Every night, I write down my own personal goals for the next day. I also have a scheduling book that helps me stay on track with how many clients I have. And, I never skip making time for myself. I always make sure that I fit in my own workout, whatever it may be, and I never skip that.

Chambers:

What advice would you give to someone who is just starting to come up as a trainer, and wants to be more successful? What advice would you give them?

McKay:

The advice that I would give someone else who is trying to become a trainer is that the most important thing is to be a good listener. Remember that you're the one that they're looking up to. You need to stay focused and motivated. That's what they need every single time that they come and see you.

They don't want to hear you talk about your own personal problems. They want to come to you as an outlet and to help them get over their stress. And to also make sure that you're having fun while training!

Chambers:

What inspires you?

McKay:

It inspires me when I see other people who are working hard. I always want to be that person working hard and trying to reach my goals. I'm inspired by being a good mentor. I want people to know that they can look up to me, and that I'm a positive role model in one way, or another.

Chambers:

What is the greatest reward of doing what you do?

McKay:

The greatest reward I have, is that I have an opportunity to help change 8–10 people's lives every day.

Chambers:

How long do you see yourself doing this type of work?

McKay:

I see myself being a trainer forever – it may not be fulltime, but it's in me, and it's something that I will do for the rest of my life.

Chambers:

For you, what is the greatest risk you've ever taken, and was it worth it?

McKay:

I think the greatest risk I've taken so far is saying "Yes" to the opportunity to move out here. Leaving in all my amazing clients, friends and boyfriend in Seattle and coming to California not really knowing anyone and basically starting life over. It has been well worth it, I've become a better person because of it.

Chambers:
If you could do anything you knew would not fail, what would you do?

McKay:
If I knew I could be anything in the world, and I knew that I would not fail, I would want to be an Olympic track 'n field athlete. My coaches have always told me that I have the heart of a true Olympic athlete. Unfortunately the rest of it didn't quite work out, but just hearing them say that was enough for me to feel like one and that's just fine!

Chambers:
If you could give any advice to somebody, what would it be?

McKay:
If I could share any advice with anyone, it would be, "Always be true to yourself and stay strong to your beliefs, and then you won't fail at anything… as long as you stay true to who you are and what you believe in, you'll never fail. You'll always make the right decisions."

Chambers:
What type of legacy do you want to leave?

McKay:
The kind of legacy that I want to leave is that I want people to know

to never give up – always hold strong to your dreams, never lose sight of your dreams, and go after every dream, because everyone deserves to have their dreams come true. It just takes work!

Sara J. McKay
(425) 443-3710

www.sarajmckay.com
Sara@sarajmckay.com

Chapter 11

Jason Cotter
Real Estate Investor/Coach

Davie E Chambers (Chambers):
Jason you are very success real estate entrepreneur, what does it take in the real estate world to become a good leader?

Jason Cotter (Cotter):
I consider myself to be the type of person willing to put a lot of time and effort into what I do. I like to be able to offer somebody help whenever they need. I try to put forth every effort into helping people without half mast consideration for other people's views, opinions or interests. I'm not a picky guy, or a person that judges because I be-

lieve that in this business there is always a possibility someone you judge can end up to be a friend or someone who can help me in the future.

Chambers:

How do you define success?

Cotter:

I define success not by money, but by achievement. Achieving a goal can be running a marathon, or getting the greatest job. Success comes from your heart, and when you've succeeded, your heart will left you know.

Chambers:

When times are tough, how do you stay focused?

Cotter:

When times are tough, I just look at the stuff most important to me. Not the material things, but the mental things. My three kids, my wife and my goals of making there lives better are what is most important to me.

Chambers:

What is the secret combination to finding success in what you do?

Cotter:

Just do not give up. There is always a chance that the moment you give up, you could have been one step away from the greatest real estate opportunity. As long as you never give up, you will achieve success.

Chambers:

When you get discouraged, what techniques do you use to pull yourself through?

Cotter:

I stop, take a look at the object or problem in front of me, analyze it, figure out why I'm becoming stressed or discouraged, and I take control of it. A big part of it is my family. When I look at them it becomes clear to me why I am doing this, and I know in my heart that it is going to pay off in the end.

Chambers:

What inspired you to get into real estate?

Cotter:

What inspired me to do real estate is the money, the ability to do what I want, when I want, and helping people. I have a big heart, and in real estate you can either be greedy, or you can be willing to help people. What inspires me is being able to help younger couples, and give them chances no one else will give them in life.

Chambers:

What do most people not know about the real estate industry that you have already mastered?

Cotter:

That anybody can do it. You do not have to be a genius to sell real estate. You just got to have the will and the heart. It is not an easy industry but if you are willing to put your mind, your heart, your soul into it, you can achieve anything in the world.

Chambers:

How do you channel fear into productivity? When you are feeling down, you feeling exhausted and frustrated, how do you channel that into productivity?

Cotter:

When I am scared and don't know what to do I take a second look at why I am doing this. I analyze why I am in real estate and I get very clear on my goals and what I want. I know that sooner or later I am going to come out of it, so I take a second look at things, but never give up.

Chambers:

Have you a mentor to help you become successful?

Cotter:

Yes, having someone to call when I am down and having someone to call when I am just up. Just having someone to call that will listen to how my day went whether good or bad. Even the most successful people need someone to call at the end of the day.

Chambers:

When someone is trying to find a mentor, what should they look for?

Cotter:

They should look for someone with there absolute best interests in mind. Someone willing to go the extra mile for them. A lot of people are only willing to go so far for others. Some will let you go as soon as they realize your doing better than they are.

Chambers:

Let us say someone who is reading this and they are successful and they are going to become a mentor to someone else, what should they do and how should they act to be a mentor?

Cotter:

As a mentor it doesn't take much to take a minute before your day is over, to give your student a call and encourage them to stay in the game. A lot of people tend to want to give up easy. I think you should really stay on top of the person you are mentoring and always offer encouragement to those in need. As long as you keep their spirits up, they will never quit.

Chambers:

At times, all of us have quit something. With your industry and being in real estate and being as successful as you are, what would you tell someone on the verge of quitting and giving up?

Cotter:

If you quit, you do not know how close to success you could have been. You could have missed your opportunity. If you give up, you are never going to know if you could have made it.

Chambers:

Have there been times that in your world that you wanted to quit and you persevered and went through it?

Cotter:

Half the time you get discouraged. You get frustrated, people buy you out. There are a lot of people that are in it for themselves, there are a lot of people that are in it for the money, but I know that what I am doing. When I go out there and make deals, I am doing it for the people who haven't made it yet. I'm doing it for the people that need a break, and I am willing to give it to them. I'm not just looking to get filthy rich.

Chambers:

What advice would you give someone who is just staring in real estate and wants to break into it?

Cotter:

Find a good person, grab a hold of their coat tails, and hang on. It is a bumpy ride but if you are willing to go through it, there are so many goals and achievements out there, it's unreal. Just never give up. No matter how hard and no matter how much it seems like it's never going to work out, just never quit.

Chambers:

What inspires you?

Cotter:

Waking up every morning, looking at my three kids and wife thinking, they are not going to have the life I had when I was younger, and that my kids will be in a better place every day than what they were.

Chambers:

What gave you the desire to get into real estate originally?

Cotter:

Time freedom, being able to do what I want, and being able to help people. Again, my heart is out to help people. Before I was in real estate, I was gone all the time and my kids would never see me. Even though it's a job, it still takes your time. In real estate I am able to make my own schedule and make as much money as I want to make, not as much as my employer wants me to make.

Chambers:

What are some of the greatest rewards you have had from your business?

Cotter:

Knowing I didn't have the money, I knew it was going to be hard to get the first deal. When the bank said "yes" for a fourteen unit apartment complex that I had never pictured myself getting, I was so happy I broke down in tears.

Chambers:

What is the greatest risk you had ever taken and was it worth it?

Cotter:

I feel that the greatest risk I have ever taken was having three kids. It is hard to raise kids, especially in today's society, but every penny is worth waking up and seeing their beautiful faces.

Chambers:

If you can do anything and you knew you would not fail, what would you do?

Cotter:

I would buy as many houses as I can and I would help all the people I know that need a break. I would offer homes to single parents and people that have been down and out. I would be able to give them homes for way under market value.

Chambers:

If you could share any advice with someone, what would it be?

Cotter:

My advice for somebody would be, no matter how hard your life has been, no matter how many people dislike you, never quit. If you put your mind, heart and soul into anything you do, you can do it. No matter what it is, if you never give up, you will always achieve your goal as long as you never quit. It can be anything from being a school teacher, to being the president, if you want it bad enough, never give up, and never let someone discourage you by telling you "you can't do it," because the minute you believe you can't do it is the minute you are going to lose it, and miss out on your goal.

Chambers:

What type of legacy do you want to leave?

Cotter:

Here is a guy that is willing to do anything and everything for everybody else. He is willing to help anybody and everybody out. If somebody is new in the business, he is willing to help them out to get started. If somebody needs a loan, somebody needs anything that has to do with real estate that he is willing to lift his hand not looking for anything. He gives from his heart.

Jason Cotter
Real Estate Investor

34184 Countyline Rd #91
Yucaipa CA 92399
909-725-2178

cotterjason28@yahoo.com

Chapter 12

Woody Woodward
Film-maker, Author, Life Strategist

David E. Chambers (Chambers):
How did you get started in doing what you do?

Woody Woodward (Woodward):
It all started a couple of years ago – I dropped out of high school when I was 16. I was millionaire at 26, and flat broke at 27. I was always fascinated with how people could lose everything, and then make it all back. In a short five year-span, we built a mortgage and real estate firm in seven different states, we had 50 loan officers, and

were generating about $30 million a year.

Chambers:

That is an amazing story! How did you get into writing books and producing movies?

Woodward:

I got into writing books because of my background. I was fascinated with dropouts – how they could fail and succeed, and go back and forth. So, after we had the mortgage company going successfully, I took some time off and read over a thousand biographies of 'who's whos' and how they overcame their obstacles and challenges. In that process, I decided to write a book called 'Millionaire Dropouts'.

It has now led to set of book series called 'Millionaire Dropouts'. It's been published and is on Amazon and Barnes and Noble. It was even referred to by the Forbes Book Club as a Book Club Recommendation.

Chambers:

What is 'Millionaire Dropouts' all about?

Woodward:

'Millionaire Dropouts' is about how people with no education and very little means can go on to overcome obstacles. I've always been fascinated with trying to figure out what is in someone's mind that allows them – even though they've repeatedly fallen down–to get back up and get started. And in the process of writing 'Millionaire Dropouts', I discovered something that I call the 'Law of Importance'.

Chambers:

What is the 'Law of Importance'?

Woodward:

The 'Law of Importance' states "All human behavior is governed by what makes one feel important." And what makes you feel important is different than what is important to you.

So, for example, family may be important to you, but family may not make you feel important. That feeling of importance is when you feel on top of the world. We all have our good days, and our bad days, but we have those peak moments when we feel absolutely incredible! We feel on top of the world, almost as if the world could not get better. That is what is meant by 'a feeling of importance'.

We all have it. It doesn't matter whether you're young or old, whether you're the President of the United States, a famous celebrity or a professional athlete... we all have this feeling of importance. And it is this feeling of importance that drives us from within to do what we do.

Chambers:

After you discovered the 'Law of Importance', what transpired? What took place in your life that led you to producing movies and writing additional books?

Woodward:

I was in the middle of writing 'Millionaire Dropouts' when I discovered the 'Law of Importance', and I realized that I had to finish that first so that I could go on to this next project that kept me up at night. I was so excited to get involved in it!

After finishing 'Millionaire Dropouts', I decided to start interviewing people. I interviewed over a thousand people, trying to figure out what made them feel important. And in the process, I realized that everybody has at least five different things that make them feel important. It's different for every person – it's like your emotional fingerprint. It could be something as simple as 'I feel important when I'm accepted by others', or 'I feel important when I'm shopping', or 'I feel important when I'm being creative', or 'I feel important when I'm an individual'. It's different for every single person. It is that feeling of importance that drives you to do what you do.

I refer to those five things that make you feel important as your 'Five I's'. The I stands for Importance. The Five I's are really how you dictate your good days and bad days. If two or more of your I's are getting met simultaneously, you have a positive peak in emotion. So, if you have an I of creativity, and an I of being an individual, and you're painting and creating, you will feel on top of the world! The rest of the world has nothing to do with it. Money has nothing to do with it. Whether you're being recognized by other people, or whether you are better than someone else, has nothing to do with it.

Now, the flipside is that if two or more of your I's are being offended simultaneously, you'll have a negative drop in attitude, more so than a normal day. so, if you have an I of creativity, and an I of being an individual – it makes you feel important when you're independent – and you're busy working and can't find the free time to go home and paint, or be creative, and your boss is yelling at you, emotionally, you have this deep valley of frustration. Sometimes, you're in depression.

Chambers:

Since you've discovered the 'Law of Importance', where has your life led you to now?

Woodward:

Life has been an amazing rollercoaster ride since I discovered the 'Law of Importance.' We've had opportunities to speak around the country, we've done business in Thailand, Ireland, North America... you name it, and we've been there. We've been everywhere! In the process, there's an associate of mine who's working with the United Nations on helping them develop techniques that will be presented to help them reach their millennium goals. One of those is a documentary on the 'Law of Importance' and how it works. So, we did that and in the process, I thought, "You know what? We need to do a documentary for everybody."

We took two years and a budget of about $1 million and developed this incredible movie called I-ology. You can see a trailer of the movie on the website www.iologymovie.com. After making this movie, it was incredible – we've now got distribution overseas and it's being translated in multiple different languages. What's most rewarding for me, is that people are starting to get it. They understand that it is universally accepted, that everybody has a feeling of importance.

In fact, some of the greatest minds like Dr. John Dewy have said, "The deep urge of human nature is the desire to be important". Dr. David J. Schwartz said, "Man's most compelling non-biological hunger, is the desire to be important." Even the Father of American Psychology – William James said, "The deepest principle in human nature is the craving to be appreciated. Everybody has this feeling of importance."

Once again, it's not negative. It's not about being more important than somebody else. It's that feeling that you get when you just know that you're on top of the world. That is your emotional fingerprint.

Chambers:
What inspires you?

Woodward:
I'm inspired by helping other people realize that they are important – they have a feeling of importance, and when they live that that internally, from within, they have the ability to accomplish anything.

Chambers:
What makes a good leader?

Woodward:
A good leader is somebody who, from an internal state, can direct an external movement. This means, a good leader is someone who is not looking for validation from their peers, who internally has a moral compass of where they want to take their business, and their relationships, and they lead from within, and in the process, externally, those around them, stand up and notice. They want to make a difference in their own lives, because that person has gone out and made a difference.

Chambers:
How do you define success?

Woodward:

I define success by truly knowing who you are, having a complete identity of what you are and who you are, and living that from within. You are not looking for validation, acceptance or recognition. When you have that feeling, where internally, you know right from wrong, you know how to get what you want from life... that, to me, is true success.

Chambers:

What are your goals for the upcoming year?

Woodward:

My goal for the upcoming year is to get the Law of Importance to out to the masses. We're in the middle of doing a book right now, on the Law of Importance, we've already done a movie on the Law of Importance and we're working on a lot of different projects. I want to get the Law of Importance out to multiple continents, to multiple people and to public and national television, so that everybody understands what makes them feel important and how to live that from within, so that they're not constantly bombarded by external forces.

Chambers:

If you could do anything, and you knew you would not fail, what would you do?

Woodward:

I am happy to say that I would do exactly what I am doing right now. I don't feel that I can fail. I don't worry about failing. Many people are fearful that if they fail, they'll lose everything. I'm happy to lose everything because I'm doing what I want to do. I'm doing my life's work! Discovering the Law of Importance and helping other people understand what makes them feel important – to me, I can never fail in that arena.

Chambers:
What advice would you give to a budding entrepreneur?

Woodward:
The advice I would give a budding entrepreneur is that it is crucial for them to follow their dreams, no matter what business they're starting, no matter what desires they have. When they go out into the world, if they are worried about what other people and what others are going to say, they're never going to be successful. As a budding entrepreneur, you have got to follow your dream. You've got to go for your passion, your hopes, your goals, your dreams and your aspirations – you have to move forward in your life. If you don't, you'll spend a lifetime regretting that, and wishing you did.

Chambers:
What is the greatest risk you have ever taken, and was it worth it?

Woodward:
The greatest risk I have ever taken was leaving the mortgage company and following my heart into the Law of Importance, and risking everything I have to make this known. And it was absolutely worth it! If I were to make one penny, or even if I were to go completely bankrupt, knowing that I spent my life trying to help other people, it is a life worth living and it's totally worth everything I've ever done.

Chambers:

What type of a legacy do you want to leave?

Woodward:

The legacy that I want to leave is to give people the tools with which they can find the ability within, to live their life the way they have chosen to live it – not to be wishy-washy, not to be afraid, not to live in fear. They will live with a moral compass that directs them for good, every single day.

Woody Woodward
Law Of Importance

39252 Winchester Rd #107-430
Murrieta, CA 92563

Your Personal Interview

What does it take to be a leader?

....

....

....

....

....

....

....

When times are tough how do you stay focused? How do you define success?

....

....

....

....

....

....

....

....

....

What is the greatest risk you have ever taken and was it worth it?

....

....

....

....

....

....

....

....

....

What is the secret combination to finding success in your line of work?

....

....

....

....

....

....

....

....

What inspired you to go into this type of business?

....

....

....

....

....

....

....

....

What do most people not know about your industry?

....

....

....

....

....

....

....

....

How do you define failure?

....

....

....

....

....

....

....

....

....

What is the difference between giving up and failing at something?

....

....

....

....

....

....

....

....

....

How has having a mentor helped you to be successful?

....

....

....

....

....

....

....

....

....

When someone is finding a mentor what should they look for?

....

....

....

....

....

....

....

....

....

....

What has been your greatest Ah-ha moment in business?

....

....

....

....

....

....

....

....

....

When did you fire your boss? What was it like? Where you scared?

....

....

....

....

....

....

....

....

How do you channel FEAR into productivity?

....

....

....

....

....

....

....

....

....

What strategies do you use to fight time management?

....

....

....

....

....

....

....

....

....

....

What advice and encouragement would you give to a budding entre-
preneur?

....

....

....

....

....

....

....

....

What inspires you?

....

....

....

....

....

....

....

Why do you do what you do?

....

....

....

....

....

....

....

....

....

....

What do you like best about what you do?

....

....

....

....

....

....

....

....

If you could be a part in another business other than what you are in now what would it be and why?

....

....

....

....

....

....

....

....

What type of legacy do you want to leave?

....

....

....

....

....

....

....

If you could share any advice with someone what would it be?

....

....

....

....

....

....

....

....

....

....

....

Quotes of Success

Inspire your mind to achieve

"It takes as much energy to wish as it does to plan."
– Eleanor Roosevelt

"Don't waste your effort on a thing that results in a petty triumph unless you are satisfied with a life of petty issues."
– John D. Rockerfeller, Industrialist

"Always bear in mind that your own resolution to succeed is more important than any other."
– Abraham Lincoln, 16th US President

Count your blessings, not your problems. And remember: amateurs built the ark... professionals built the Titanic.

- Unknown

"I have learned to use the word "impossible" with the greatest caution."

– Werner von Braun, Engineer

"The ultimate measure of a man is not where he stands in moments of comfort, but where he stands in times of challenge and controversy."

– Martin Luther King, Jr., Clergyman, Civil Rights Leader

"All life is a chance. So take it! The person who goes furthest is the one who is willing to do and dare."

– Dale Carnegie, Author

"Every idea you present must be something you could get across easily at a cocktail party with strangers."

– Jack Welch – GE Chief Executive

"Only those who risk going too far can possibly find out how far one can go."

– T. S. Eliot – Poet

He who loses wealth loses much; he who loses a friend loses more; but he who loses his courage loses all.

-Miguel de Cervantes

"If we all did the things we are capable of doing, we would literally astound ourselves."

– Thomas Edison – Inventor

"The mediocre teacher tells. The good teacher explains. The superior teacher demonstrates. The great teacher inspires."

– William Ward – Texas Wesleyan University Administrator

"It is our choices . . . that show what we truly are, far more than our abilities."

– J. K. Rowling, Children's Book Author

"Whether you think that you can, or that you can't you are usually right."

– Henry Ford, Carmaker

It's time to start living the life you've imagined.

- Henry James

"Even the fear of death is nothing compared to the fear of not having lived authentically and fully."

– Frances Moore Lappe

"Leaders are visionaries with a poorly developed sense of fear and no concept of the odds against them. They make the impossible happen."

– Robert Jarvik

"Enthusiasm is the greatest asset in the world. It beats money and power and influence. It is no more or less than faith in action."

– Henry Chester, writer

"Nothing great has ever been achieved except by those who dared believe that something inside them was superior to circumstances."

– Bruce Barton, advertising executive

"There's only one way to succeed in anything, and that is to give everything."

– Vince Lombardi, football coach

"He who has a "why" to live can bear with almost any "how."

– Friedrich Nietzsche, philosopher

"Eliminate the time between the idea and the act, and your dreams will become realities."

-Dr. Edward L Kramer,

"There is only one success – to be able to spend your life in your own way.

-Christopher Morley

"The real measure of success is the number of experiments that can be crowded into 24 hours."

– Thomas Edison, inventor

"There is no passion to be found playing small – in settling for a life that idles than the one you are capable of living."

– Nelson Mandela, civil rights leader